When mothers must work . . .

When mothers must work . . .

Carolyn Sedgwick

When Mothers Must Work

Printed in the United States of America
ISBN: 0-88368-208-7

For Dan who loves me enough to let me grow.
May our next thirty years be as beautiful as the first.

Contents

Part Two

Finding, Evaluating, and Keeping Quality Day Care

Preface

Difficult decisions and compromises are part of a working woman's life. But no mother wants to compromise when it comes to her family. We want the best for them, especially when it comes to child care.

When Mothers Must Work deals in part with the general problems that working mothers face, but good child care is the key to making working *work*. When you feel secure about your children's well-being, all else is "doable."

This book is the culmination of my dreams to help mothers solve their day care problems. It is based on my personal experience as a mother, grandmother, and day care provider. I have also collected information and experiences from other caregivers, child care professionals, and parents.

I hope *When Mothers Must Work* will make your child care choices easier and happier to live with. I present it to you with the prayer that the choices you make will give you peace and joy.

Part One

How to Make Working Work for You and Your Family

1

A Woman's Priorities

Setting the Record Straight

Today, working mothers are accepted as a fact in modern America. No longer does society dictate that the woman's place is only in the home. As society has changed so has the way mothers view going to work.

In my mother's generation women got married and stayed home to raise a family. My generation worked before marriage and up until children were born. Then we stayed home until the kids started school or were even in high school before we returned to work. My daughter's generation went to work after school or college and continued working through child rearing.

While the changes in society have given us more choices, they have also added to the confusion. One day the woman's role is in the home, and the next it's best to be on the job. First public opinion tells us only mothers should care for their children, then they say others can do it just as well.

About the time we adapt to the current lifestyle trends, someone decides we should be doing the opposite! Thank goodness, we as Christians don't have to depend on the world to set standards for us. We can make our choices according to the unchanging principles of God's Word.

What Does the Bible Say?

As Christians we stand on the firm foundation of faith—not on the shifting sands of society's dictates. We have God's wisdom to help us make the choices that are best for us as individuals. By examining our options in light of Scripture, we can know *how* and *what* to choose.

God's Word challenges us not to "conform any longer to the pattern of this world," but to be "transformed by the renewing" of our minds. Then we will be able "to test and approve what God's will is—his good, pleasing and perfect will" (Romans 12:2).

The issue for Christian mothers who want to, or have to, work is not whether it is accepted according to the world's standards, but whether it is the "perfect will of God" for them.

No where does the Bible directly command, "Mothers, thou shalt not work." In fact, the virtues of working are extolled in Scripture. The woman written about in Proverbs 31 has been held up as an example of godly womanhood: "She watches over the affairs of her household and does not eat the bread of idleness" (Proverbs 31:27). Throughout the Bible women are praised for their labors.

Motherhood itself is a full-time job that requires tremendous skill, endless energy, and unceasing prayer. The world says it's okay to work outside the home after motherhood. But what does God's Word tell us?

In the early Church, a respected woman was described as one who "has been faithful to her husband, and is well-known for her good deeds, such as bringing up children, showing hospitality, washing the feet of the saints, helping those in trouble and devoting herself to all kinds of good deeds." Also, younger women were encouraged to "have children, to manage their homes and to give the enemy no opportunity for slander." (See 1 Timothy 5:8-14.)

According to Scripture, a woman's priorities revolve around her responsibilities to marry, bear children, and manage her household. The home is the woman's work assignment—whether it is B.C. (before children) or A.D. (after debt). The issue is not whether she should work or not but whether she is first fulfilling her responsibilities to God, husband, and children as outlined in God's Word.

How then does a mother decide whether, or when, to work outside the home? Work is a necessity for some women, especially single parents and those who have no other financial choice. But when there is no clear necessity, the decision to work must be a careful balancing of financial, family, personal, and spiritual needs. The following guidelines may help you make the right decision for you and your family.

Following the Chain of Command

Magazine articles, newspapers, books, and TV talk shows discuss both the rewards and problems of being a working mother. The Supermom myth has given way to a more balanced approach to women's roles, and the media now encourages us to relax, enjoy our lives, and accept our limitations. Because working mothers are now accepted, we are supported and encouraged to do our best—at work and at home.

That's fine and commendable, but we must return to the question of priorities. God created the family, and He meant it to work as a unit for each individual's good and for His glory.

God brought man and woman together to bear children and raise a family: "Male and female he created them. God blessed them and said to them, 'Be fruitful, and increase in number' " (Genesis 1:27, 28). If the family is so important to God, then we must make sure ours is operating according to the principles set forth in His Word.

The family structure is defined for us in Ephesians 5:22-33: "For the husband is the head of the wife as Christ is the head of the church . . . Now as the church submits to Christ, so also wives should submit to their husbands in everything."

The biblical chain of command—*God-husband-wife-child*—is still in effect today. The rest of this passage in Ephesians tells the husband to "love his wife as he loves himself," and the wife is exhorted to "respect her husband."

Mutual love and respect for each other's needs, concerns, and well-being are the cornerstone of a good marriage. That is especially true in two-paycheck marriages where job demands are added to the already heavy responsibility of raising a family and creating a home.

A husband who loves his wife as himself will work with her in making the decision whether to work or not to work. He will also be there to assist with the after-effects of that decision. A wife who reveres her husband will respect his opinions and be willing to submit to his decisions.

A Decision You Can Both Live With

Communication in every area of marriage should always be direct and clear. In making the decision whether a mother should work or not, nothing short of total, prayerful honesty between husband and wife will do.

When Betty couldn't stretch the family's income to meet basic living expenses, she discussed with her husband the possibility of her getting a job. She *thought* he agreed that a second income would be helpful.

It wasn't until she'd been working for a month that Betty realized something was terribly wrong at home. In spite of the increased income, no one was really happy—least of all her husband, Al. When she confronted him about their deteriorating home life, she was surprised to hear that he actually hated her working outside the home.

Betty had gotten a job to help take the financial pressure off Al. She really didn't want to work outside the home, but she saw it as the only solution to their problems. Al had agreed to her working, but he hadn't told her it was because he felt he'd failed the family financially. Although they had supposedly discussed the initial decision, neither had been truly open about their feelings.

Once Al and Betty started talking more honestly, they discovered they both wanted the same thing—for Betty to be home full time. Betty quit her job and started doing dressmaking for extra income. Al put in for all the overtime he could get, and the entire family worked at balancing the budget.

"The extra money just wasn't worth the stress," Betty said. "It wasn't easy, but we managed and everyone is much happier with me at home."

That reminds me of a verse from *The Living Bible*: "A dry crust eaten in peace is better than steak every day along with argument and strife" (Proverbs 17:1). If your working outside the home only creates tension and strife in the family, you may need to reconsider your priorities and opt for peace instead of prosperity.

Joan's husband, Bud, didn't want her to work—*ever*. While Joan wasn't interested in working when her children were younger, as they grew older and less dependent on her she became restless. The children had their friends and activities, Bud had his job, and most of Joan's friends had returned to work or moved away. Although her nest wasn't empty yet, it was mighty lonely between nine and five each day.

Bud realized Joan needed an interest of her own, but that didn't change his mind about her working. Because he loved his wife and wanted her to be happy, they discussed ways for Joan to fill her time in a satisfying way. When their church's preschool announced they needed teachers' aides, Joan and Bud both agreed they'd found a solution to their problem. Joan loves working with the teachers, and Bud loves his contented and happy wife!

When Working Doesn't Work

Today's woman has the freedom to choose to work, but sometimes we forget that she should also have the freedom to choose not to work.

Some women just don't like working outside the home. Their husbands may want them to work, their children do well when mom's not at home, their jobs may be fantastic, yet they long to be back home in front of the range. Some don't mind working part-time, short term, or for only specific periods in their lives, but a full-time job makes them miserable.

Sometimes working doesn't work because the time isn't right. Mothers of young children often regret the decision to work when they realize the turmoil it creates in the lives of their little ones. Waiting until the children are in school full time has advantages but may shake the stability of a child's secure home environment. A wife who works while her husband furthers his education may feel needed and fulfilled at the time but later resent having to work when their financial situation has improved.

Some women work for the wrong reasons. A mother who gets a job because everyone else is working has her priorities out of order. If a woman goes to work out of fear—because society says she needs job security and financial protection against a possible divorce—both she and her family may regret her decision in the end.

Before deciding to get a job or returning to work after motherhood, prayerfully consider the priorities outlined in God's Word. While some priorities are clearly defined, others are a matter of personal conviction.

As a Christian wife and mother, you are responsible before God to seek to please the Lord and your family before all others. If you can do that within the confines of a full or part-time job, then you will have the peace and assurance that working is God's will for you. Set the record straight in your own heart, and you won't have to worry about what society thinks.

2

To Work or Not to Work

Questions You Need to Ask Yourself

Before making the final decision to get a job, you need to determine *why* you are considering going to work outside the home.

Some women choose to work in order to provide their families with a better lifestyle. Others are beguiled by the world to believe that work (or the money it supplies) is an essential ingredient for a happy and prosperous life. The media tells us that a house, two cars, the latest video equipment, and a two week vacation every year are necessities no American should be without.

But should we as Christian women pursue outside employment solely for those "extras" a second paycheck can provide? There is nothing wrong with wanting to upgrade our lifestyles, but we must be careful to use God's yardstick rather than the world's measure.

Jesus said, "Watch out! Be on guard against all kinds of greed; a man's life does not consist in the abundance of his possessions" (Luke 12:15).

As Christians we need to be careful about comparing our lifestyle to the one portrayed by commercial television and magazine advertising. Our hearts and minds must continually be on guard against developing the "keep-up-with-the-Jones" mentality.

Need or Greed?

God has promised to supply all our needs. The problem comes in discerning what is a need and what is greed. Clothing your children in the latest designer fashions may seem like a desperate need to them, but what does God's Word say?

> Do not worry, saying, "What shall we eat?" or "What shall we drink?" or "What shall we wear?" For the pagans run after all these things, and your heavenly Father knows that you need them. But seek first his kingdom and his righteousness, and all these things will be given to you as well—Matthew 6:31-33.

Janet's family can manage on her husband's income. But they would like to live in a nicer neighborhood, where the schools are better and their children would be away from some of the bad influences they are now subjected to. A move, however, would necessitate Janet's return to work.

I am reminded that God told Moses to take His people out of Egypt and away from its wicked influences. Lot was also told to take his family and leave Sodom and Gomorrah. We, too, have a responsibility to protect our families from today's evils. A move to a safer neighborhood may be necessary.

Renting rather than buying may accomplish the same goal without Janet's having to work outside the home. Other solutions may be working part time or moving to a different and less expensive community.

Ann would like to go to work to upgrade their mostly comfortable lifestyle. She's tired of driving well-used cars and buying secondhand furniture. A job isn't a necessity, but it would be great to have a sofa that didn't need strategically-placed throw pillows to hide the worn spots.

Ann's family will have to compare the advantages of a job that would allow them to have some of the nicer things they'd like against the disadvantages of her working outside the home.

In Christian families, the motives behind Mom's working should be prayerfully and honestly considered. We need to ask ourselves: Are we following the world's lust for bigger, better material possessions? Or are our needs reasonable?

You may want to make a list of the reasons you are going to work and honestly evaluate your motives. See if they line up with God's Word and ask the Lord to reveal any hidden areas of pride and greed. God wants to bless and prosper your family, but He wants to do it in a way that is best for all concerned.

Do You Need to Work?

Some women find working outside the home personally satisfying. They want to work, and they enjoy the challenges of a job. Others find that the social stimulation of the workplace helps them function better when they are at home.

Emma wanted to stay home with her young daughter. But when her strong-willed mother-in-law moved into the household, her doctor prescribed an outside job to ease the tensions at home. Emma's newfound job became a refuge that raised her self-esteem and made it easier to cope with the difficult but unavoidable home situation. Her four-year-old thrived in a good pre-school.

For Pat working was a necessity. As a recently divorced young mother, she had no choice but to return to college, complete her degree, and get a job. Pat had moved back home with her parents when she started college, and her mother agreed to keep little Amy during the day.

Recently Pat told me, "Going back to school and getting a job helped me keep my sanity during an emotionally draining time. The Lord provided in every way, and my daughter benefited from my mother's strict discipline."

For Lynne the answer she prayerfully sought was not the one she got.

"I was a teacher before I had my family," she said. "I stayed home during the children's early years because this is what my husband and I felt God wanted for us."

One day Lynne spent her morning in prayer, asking God if she could now return to her career. The children were all in school full time, and she wanted to teach again. While she hadn't received a clear answer, Lynne left the matter with the Lord, knowing that He would send one—not on *her* timetable but on His own. She rose from her knees and walked across the bedroom to peer out the upstairs window.

"There coming down the street was my son," she said. "Since it was during school hours, I ran down to meet him."

Today Lynne doesn't even recall what had sent her youngster scurrying home in the middle of the morning. "If I had been at work, I wouldn't have been there to deal with his problem," she said. "Some problems can wait, but others need immediate attention. What if he hadn't come home because he would have known I wasn't there? The possibilities are endless, and disturbing."

Lynne found other ways to meet her personal needs for stimulation, and she's still waiting to go back to work.

"God will let me know when the time is right," she said with confidence.

Can You Handle It?

God created each of us with different abilities. It's naive to assume that every mother can handle work and home with time left over to be a loving wife plus faithful church worker.

We need to examine our own capabilities and resources before making a decision to work outside the home. The woman described in Proverbs 31 was a superb manager and a wonderful model for all women. But some women have more energy than others; some are more organized than others; and some find they need eleven-day weeks to get from Sunday to Sunday without drowning in diapers and dust.

Do you have the energy and organization necessary to tackle working at home and on a job? Will you be able to hire occasional help with housework if necessary? Do you have the family support to keep the house from falling apart? If you don't, do you have the ability to ignore the unfolded laundry and the soft-focus view through less than sparkling windows?

You need to ask yourself: Can I handle working with the temperament and personality God has given me? If you aren't sure, get a temporary part-time job first as an experiment. Work at a department store during the Christmas season or apply to a secretarial service. You'll soon know whether working is right for you.

Examine your personal needs prayerfully and let God give you the strength to work or not to work according to His will for you. If you trust in the Lord, delight yourself in Him, and commit your ways to Him, He will "give you the desires of your heart" (Psalm 37:4).

How Will Working Affect Your Children?

Most contemporary Christian families feel that Mom's working only becomes a problem when her job interferes with her primary role as wife and mother. Your children's needs should be a primary consideration in your decision to work or not to work.

Will your infant be well-cared for by a babysitter? How will your shy toddler be affected by going to day care? Will your school-age child be lost without you to come home to each day?

You may think that leaving adolescent children on their own is okay, but they are vulnerable to peer pressure that might lead them into situations too hot to handle.

"I went to work when my girls were teenagers because I felt they could manage on their own," said Marianne. "But I found out one had been cutting school regularly and the other had her boyfriend over every afternoon. I quit my job immediately!"

My own teenage son would have been delighted if I'd gone to work once he reached junior high age. I don't know what mischief he had planned, but even good kids can get carried away by temptation if given the time and place. I decided to head him off at the pass! Instead of going to work, I stayed home and prayed I'd have enough bread on hand when he and his friends stopped by for unexpected lunches.

Before plunging ahead into the working world, make sure the entire family has a clear understanding of what changes will take place and how their lives will be affected. Your husband and children should share in an open discussion of all the issues—from added responsibilities to wake up times. Without the support of the entire family, working may bring confusion if not complete chaos to your household.

Do You Really Want to Work?

If you are going to work because you *want* to rather than because you *have* to, you are blessed. When working is a choice rather than a necessity, the problems that do arise from your taking a job won't be complicated by feelings of guilt and frustration.

The first time I went to work after becoming a parent, I was living with my sister and her family while my husband was on overseas military duty. I got a job to create a nest egg to see us through the transition from military to civilian life. When Dan got settled in a job, I planned to stay home again. Because it was a chosen and temporary situation, and because my sister would be caring for our infant daughter, it was easier for me to go off to work each day.

Years later, when we had three children and I had to get a job because of financial difficulties, I cried all the way to work for a week. I didn't want to work; I wanted to be home. The child care arrangements were not satisfactory; the children didn't like my not being there when they came home from school; and my husband hated hassling with the kid's problems when I wasn't available.

I lasted on the job six weeks—not because the problems were insurmountable but because I really didn't want to, or have to, work badly enough to make my working work for us. We found other alternatives to our financial problems.

The decision to quit working isn't any easier than making the choice to get a job in the first place. Each decision should be based on prayerful evaluation of your individual family's needs.

We would all like to own our own home, save for our children's college fund, and have more financial freedom to enjoy the material things in life. But we need to ask ourselves: Do the advantages of my working outweigh the disadvantages?

In some families the answer is yes. If you work because you want to, then all the hassels and aggravations won't bother you. You'll find ways to meet the many challenges of combining work and motherhood because you are doing what you feel is best for you and your family.

Determining God's Will for You

There are no easy answers to the question whether mothers should work or not. God does, however, give us guidelines for making all life's decisions. First, we must search Scripture prayerfully. Ask the Lord to show you what He wants you to do.

Second, be willing to be obedient to what God reveals to you through His Word. We don't always get the answers we want. God may say yes, no, or wait awhile.

Third, we must be willing to make sacrifices. Sometimes careers or personal desires must wait. You may have to forego the deluxe van in favor of an economy station wagon.

Fourth, we must trust in His provision for us. If God shows you that a job is right for you at this time, He will help you make the adjustments necessary to make working work. If He says "no," He will show you how to survive without that extra paycheck.

One young married woman quit her job as a nurse when she and her husband had their first child. They felt the Lord wanted them to trust Him to meet their needs. To save money for a down payment on a house, they lived for a while in Grandma's old farmhouse.

Today, with four darling girls and a beautiful new home, she told me, "When I quit my job, it was a step of faith for us. But within only a few years, the Lord blessed us, and now my husband's income is more than if both of us were working. I often wonder where we would be if we had tried to do it all ourselves."

God is faithful. You can trust Him to supply your needs—whatever they are. He can provide a job for you. Or, He can increase your husband's income while you stay home with the children and pray for God to favor and bless the work of his hands.

Don't limit God. His ways are perfect, and all you have to do is trust and obey. Besides, He's the only one who can make working work for you.

3

Choices and Changes

Keeping Your Goals in Mind

We all know what happens to even the best thought-out and carefully made plans—they change!

We underestimate. We overestimate. Circumstances change; our families change; and our jobs change. But as unruly as plans may be, we need to have them.

In one of my forays into the outside work world I thought I had foreseen all the possible problems and dealt with them before I actually got the job. My husband and I agreed it was a good time for me to go to work. My teen-aged children felt they no longer needed me at home full time. In fact, they were eager to be on their own.

In previous work experiences I had discovered that I didn't want to work full time away from my family. This time I purposely chose a small company that hired college students—most of whom wanted the evening and weekend hours that I didn't. In my interview I made it clear that I only wanted to work twenty to twenty-four hours a week, and I was hired anyway! It seemed that our plans had the Lord's blessing.

Yet within one month, the manager who had hired me was fired, and I was told I would have to work as many and whatever hours I was needed. Because our family financial situation had unexpectedly changed also, I couldn't afford to tell the new manager no. In the next six months our home and my work life went through changes that we had never anticipated.

We hadn't known the future, but God had. With His loving care we weathered all the changes and learned to cope in ways we never thought we could. In an unexpected time of transition, we learned that God "will be the sure foundation of your times, a rich store of salvation and wisdom and knowledge" (Isaiah 33:6).

Plans may not always work out "our" way, but they are still important. Having goals in mind helps you explore options and make decisions. Then if unexpected changes occur, you can adjust without totally abandoning your original objectives. Planning is a tool that will make your life easier. "We should make plans—counting on God to direct us" (Proverbs 16:9, *The Living Bible*).

Establishing Long Term Goals

A former neighbor of ours went to work to buy new drapes for her living and dining room. Two years later she didn't have the drapes, but she was still working with no chance of quitting in sight. Every time Joanne was ready to order her drapes, another appliance expired or one of the kids needed braces.

Unless you have a definite plan, you may find yourself caught up in a two-paycheck lifestyle merry-go-round that will spin you in circles instead of toward your intended objective.

When making plans, first establish your long term goals. Keep in mind *why* you went to work. Then set up the day to day details that keep a family functioning on the way to those goals. Use the planning process to focus on your needs and to set priorities.

If you went to work with a specific objective in mind—buying a house or meeting college expenses—have you set up a savings plan to achieve your goal?

If you are working to make the family budget stretch to cover living expenses, how will you spend your paycheck to meet that goal? Will you chip away at existing bills to bring them all down to manageable levels? Or will you concentrate on eliminating one large payment to ease the monthly crunch?

Have you decided to work until you reach a specific goal? Or do you want to get the finances under control, and then continue until you decide what to do next?

My mother went to work to pay off hospital bills and continued to work even after they were paid. Mama decided that the time she had worked, when added to her previous time with the company, made it worthwhile to continue until retirement.

Defining Short Term Objectives

Whatever your goals are, try to define them in a brief sentence or two. Then refine them by breaking each long term goal into specific time frames or steps to be accomplished along the way. Both financial and personal objectives are easier to attain when you set levels of achievement that lead to the ultimate goal.

A financial goal to buy a house could be divided into phase one—the down payment; phase two—building an income that will qualify you for a mortgage; and phase three—moving expenses. A personal goal may be to attain a particular job level that first requires furthering your education then actively seeking a higher position with another company.

Women who work for other than financial reasons will have different goals than those of women who need the income. A career-oriented woman may want to work toward a higher job level or a position with more responsibility. A woman who enjoys working because it is personally satisfying may want to use a current job as a stepping stone into another, more enjoyable field.

Whatever your reasons for working, your efforts will be more directed and concentrated if you establish your objectives and define your short term goals. But the secret to true success is offering them all back to the Lord and trusting Him to lead and guide you. Wise King Solomon said, "Commit to the Lord whatever you do, and your plans will succeed" (Proverbs 16:3).

What's Mine is Ours

When both spouses work, financial planning takes a different turn and can be traumatic for the husband, especially if his wife has never worked before. With another wage-earner on the scene, he may feel threatened *or* he may feel relieved. A wife who is sensitive to her husband in this area of finances will tread lightly until the ground rules are established.

Agreeing on *how* the income and expenditures should be handled is more important than *who* actually manages the finances.

Most two-income families fall into three money management categories: one, they combine both paychecks and pay bills out of a common checkbook; two, they combine paychecks for family expenses and each have a separate fund for personal use; or three, each person handles their own income and expenses.

A common hazard of an extra paycheck is believing that it will solve all your problems. Without careful planning it is easy to become lulled into false security and end up in the same financial situation you went to work to solve. Be constantly aware of how your extra income is being spent.

Make the disbursement of your new income a group project by getting your family involved in financial planning. You and your husband have made the major decisions, now include the children in some of the minor money matters. Give them a general overview of your financial goals and what you are doing to achieve them. Let their age and interests determine how much they need to know. Children can become helpers and supporters when they feel included in family plans.

If they are old enough to handle their own spending, set aside money for allowances or special treats that they can choose themselves. Allow the children to decide whether to buy their lunches at school or brown-bag it and use the savings for something else. If you include everyone in deciding whether to save for a camper or a trip to Disney World, the children will be more satisfied with the final decision.

Hidden Expenses

Before you go to work, try to estimate your working expenses, including wardrobe, transportation, and child care. Be realistic about your needs. You may plan to wear your current wardrobe, but if your new job is in an office where everyone else "dresses for success," you may find it necessary to spend whether you had planned to or not. If you start out riding public transportation but find it cumbersome and time consuming, shopping for a second car may strain the budget.

Watch for hidden expenditures. Most child care costs remain constant, but if your child's center has frequent excursions and special events that require small additional fees for admission, treats or lunches, you need to know how much to add to your budget to cover them. Contributions to office collections for gifts and the coffee kitty can quickly add up to sizeable amounts, too.

You won't be able to foresee all the unexpected expenses of working, so leave room in the budget for flexibility. When you discuss your finances, throw in enough "what ifs" to cushion your expectations. If a budget problem comes up, handle it immediately. Don't wait to see if it will take care of itself. Minor adjustments made early may help you avoid major problems later.

Periodically re-evaluate your game plans, and look at goals to see if they still meet your needs. Make adjustments to financial plans as your needs change.

No one can anticipate every possible situation, and a wise person is willing to change plans when necessary. The Bible says, "Many are the plans in a man's heart, but it is the Lord's purpose that prevails" (Proverbs 16:9). If you continually seek the Lord's will and His purpose for your working, you will eventually reach the goals that are important to you and your family.

4

Housekeeping as a Team

Positive Ways to Get Your Family Involved

"I not only bring the bacon home, I cook it and clean up the kitchen afterwards," lamented one exhausted and discouraged working mother.

When you go to work *outside* the home, the rest of the family has to go to work *inside* the home or the result will be chaos. Remind yourself that you can't do everything you did before *and* hold down a full-time job. Well, you can—but you won't be the kind of wife, mother, or employee you want to be if you try to do it all and do it alone.

Women sometimes have a difficult time letting go of their role of "housekeeper." But now that you are working and sharing the role of wage earner, you need to let your family share in the housekeeping chores.

Back to the Basics

As you settle into being a working mother, take a fresh look at what has to be done to keep your home in livable shape and then make a work plan. You may find that some chores aren't worth doing—I don't know of anyone who irons sheets anymore.

Other tasks can be simplified. Pull up your bed sheets and covers so they're not lying in a heap, pick up the dirty laundry, and then close the door on the dust bunnies in the corner. Decide what absolutely has to be done and be flexible about everything else.

To me a minimum level of housework means made beds, clean bathrooms, and a tidy kitchen—all of which can be accomplished in about thirty minutes a day. Neat closets, sparkling windows, and polished furniture are nice, but not necessary to my well-being. When things pile up and threaten my sanity, I make everyone pitch in and get things caught up fast.

Talk with your family to discover what bothers each of you the most. My husband doesn't complain unless he can't get to the sink to make his coffee. My son-in-law's standards are considerably higher. Children don't usually care whether a house is messy or immaculate. Decide together what your standard will be.

Work in teams to get what *has* to be done quickly and efficiently so you will have more time for other things. Let Dad and Sis mop floors while you and Junior get groceries. Have a race—kids against parents or boys against girls to see who can clean their bedrooms quickest.

Break up jobs into manageable segments. Instead of trying to clean house all in one day, set Monday to vacuum, Wednesday to dust, Friday to mop. Use the time you save by working efficiently as a team to do the things you enjoy individually or as a family.

How to House Train a Husband

Although more women are working full time than ever before, studies show that men still only spend twenty minutes a *week* on housework! That may have shocked the survey takers, but I doubt if it surprised any working women.

Before you blame the men, take a look at your own work habits. Were you brought up in a house where Mom waited on Dad hand and foot? Do you do everything yourself rather than ask for a helping hand? When your husband does try to help, do you do the task over again or complain he didn't do it "right?" Have you ever stopped to think that your husband may have never learned to do the simple tasks that are second nature to you?

After thirty years of marriage, I was dumfounded when my husband said he didn't know how to do dishes! He wasn't fooling—he didn't know how to wash a dish by *hand*. By the time I went to work and he started helping with household chores, we had a dishwasher. He learned to rinse, load, and turn the washer on. He also mastered unloading the dishes and putting them into the cupboard. When the dishwasher "died" and I decided not to replace it right away, he didn't know how to wash dishes without the magic of a mechanical helper.

Look at *why* you aren't getting more help at home. Did your husband help out as a child growing up? Did he ever live by himself so he had to cook, clean, and shop? Have you ever asked him to help? Are you so set in your ways that you become upset or irritated when chores don't get done how, and when, you want?

Loosen up and let your husband find his own way of doing things. So what if he folds the towels sideways or wraps the leftovers in plastic wrap because he can't find a tupperware lid? *What difference does it make?* That's the question you must learn to ask yourself—over and over again—until you finally discover that it really doesn't matter as long as the job gets done.

Real Homework

Housework is a learned process. A girl isn't born with a dustcloth in her hand anymore than boy infants come into this world gripping a wrench.

Teach your family how to do the things that are necessary to keep your home operating smoothly. Husbands should be able to handle any household job, but children should be assigned tasks suitable to their age and capabilities.

Children from two to four can pick up toys and clothing; four to six year olds can put clothing in drawers and set a simple table; children from eight to ten can take out garbage, feed pets, help put away groceries, and water house plants. After ten years of age, children are generally capable of most household chores.

Don't assume family members know how to do a task. Be prepared to explain and demonstrate even the simplest chores—and be patient! Show your children and husbands how to make a bed quickly, how to clean a room efficiently, and how to operate household appliances.

Make laundry a learning experience. Small children can practice dexterity while folding washcloths and learn colors when matching socks. Children old enough to operate complex stereo and video recorder systems can certainly cope with washing machines, clothes dryers, and automatic dishwashers. Give them the instruction manuals (if you still have them!), let them read operating directions, and then show *you* what they've learned.

Learning a task together is doubly rewarding when the time is spent sharing thoughts. Most household tasks can be done while talking. Use this time to discuss serious topics like the birds and the bees, world politics, or everyday things like what you want to plant in your spring vegetable garden. Make work-time a fun-time—tell each other ridiculous jokes, sing together, or recite poetry.

Don't be so set in your ways that you aren't open to new approaches to accomplishing a task. Husbands and children may come up with innovative ideas on how to keep house that you never considered.

Quick and Easy

How many working women spend their entire day haunted by the never-ending question: What will I fix for dinner? *What* wouldn't be so hard if you only had *time* to cook. Baked chicken is great if you have an hour and a half to prepare the meal. But what does Mom do when she gets home ten minutes before Dad, and the kids have to be at soccer practice in an hour?

Working mothers need to plan, plan, plan to keep families fed and healthy without busting the budget or spending hours in the kitchen. There is a difference between fast foods (MacDonalds and Pizza Hut) and foods that cook quickly.

Make a list of family favorites that are quick and easy. One-dish meals are marvelous for working families. Watch for new recipes in magazines, on product packages, and cookbooks specializing in casseroles and time-saving recipes. Plan menus for at least a week at a time and longer if possible.

Cook double portions to save time and work. A beef roast one night can be used in a stir fry dish for tomorrow's dinner or as sandwiches for lunches. Make triple batches of Italian meat and tomato sauce and freeze for spaghetti, lasagna, and make-your-own pizzas.

Have a few simple recipes that your husband or an older child can prepare easily. You may want to copy them onto extra-large recipe cards and include additional tips on preparation to help them.

Make a grocery list and keep it posted so family members can add things as they discover supplies are low. Make it a rule that the person who empties the cereal box, coffee canister, or shampoo bottle must write it on the shopping list.

Pinpoint hectic days and plan for them. Make a pot of beans, stew, soup, or spaghetti on Saturday and feast all day Sunday on leftovers. Go out for salad bar and hamburgers before the midweek service at church.

Kids and Cooking

Cooking is a great learning experience for children. Teachers frequently use food preparation in the classroom because it encompasses reading, following directions, math, and small motor skills. Let children watch you cook when they are small, and gradually let them ease into helping you.

My children loved getting eggs from the refrigerator, leveling flour in a cup, and stirring ingredients. By starting early, children are ready to make salads, prepare a simple casserole, or bake a cake or dessert from a mix by the time they reach their teens.

Let the kids have a say in what and how to eat and how they want to share the work. Put one person in charge of making lunches or let everyone make their own. Share cooking chores and alternate with clean up. Does the table need to be set every night? Will paper plates do on weekends? Does one person enjoy cooking enough to want to make it a regular job, or do you want to take turns preparing meals?

As children get older and have busy schedules of their own, it may not be possible to eat every meal as a family.

But make it a rule that everyone gets together for dinner more often than not.

It takes time to learn how to turn your family into an efficient housekeeping team, so don't be discouraged if your efforts yield less than perfect results. Be patient with yourself and each other, and you'll be surprised at the ways you discover to keep your house a home even when mother must work.

5

"*Routine*" *Adjustments*

Managing Transportation, Sickness, and Morning Madness

Years ago there was never any question about who took care of the children. Mothers did it all. They got their youngsters up and off to school in the morning and then welcomed them back at the end of their day. In between, mothers kept the household in apple pie order.

It was always Mom who took children to doctor's appointments and nursed them through chicken pox, tonsillitis, and tummyaches. Driving the children back and forth to school and to extra activities was just part of Mom's "job."

Even when women went to work it was understood that if a child became ill or had a doctor's appointment, it was Mommy, not Daddy, who took off work. Mother continued to serve as family chauffeur to deliver children to school, day care, birthday parties, dancing lessons, sports practice, and church outings.

In today's changing world more families are learning to make decisions based on what's best for everyone rather than on gender. Some Daddies with flexible schedules, or who can finish work at home, are just as likely to take baby for a check-up or stay home when Junior has tonsillitis.

Sometimes *who* takes off work for the children's needs depends on whose schedule is more flexible that day. One time it may be Mom who can juggle best, another day it may be Dad. Special family needs are often shared by parents who make decisions based on what works rather than on the cliche—"that's your job."

Getting Everybody There

When everyone in the family has to be a certain place at a given time, Mom often assumes the role of Director of Transportation. This may involve sitting down with your husband and children and actually drawing up a chart showing how everybody will get to and from their daily destinations.

Public transportation in large cities is often inexpensive and efficient. Check out bus, subway, and rapid transit systems to see if they will work for you. If you, your husband, and children are going in different directions, it might be better if everyone uses a separate means of transportation. One parent may use the family car, another ride the city bus, and the children take the school bus.

When children are pre-school age, it may be difficult to load them and their coats, teddy bears, and diaper bags onto public transportation. Parents may want to switch schedules to allow the one who drives the family car to take and pick up children at their day care. Even if you have two cars, trading or alternating schedules can give each parent more free time.

A second car may eat into your working income, but it is probably the best way to meet the transportation needs of a busy mother in today's two-paycheck family. A car, or two cars, is more expensive than public transportation when you add up insurance, operating costs, and maintenance. But convenience and ease may outweigh financial savings.

Two cars don't have to be a budget breaker if you shop carefully for an economical used car. Don't rush into a major purchase, thinking that a second car is your only solution. Thoroughly check out your other possible alternatives.

Car Pools and Shuttle Service

When your children are school-aged and you are unable to be home in the afternoon, other transportation factors enter in. You will need to consider how to get them to and from school and then to and from day care. Some centers offer a shuttle service back and forth to school, or you may consider on-site after-school programs. A neighborhood family day care close to schools or school bus stops helps to simplify the transportation problem.

"We have worked it out so that Gary gets the girls ready for the sitter and drives them to her house," said Kathy. "I go to work early in the morning so I'm able to get off in the afternoon and pick them up. This gives me time to be at home with the girls and keeps their routine fairly normal."

Car pooling and ride sharing are other alternatives. Check with co-workers, other working parents, and friends, family, and neighbors to see if you can work out a schedule to save time and frustration.

My daughter-in-law works three days a week. Two of those days her five-year-old is in a preschool program for three hours a day. Their new sitter can't provide transportation to and from the preschool, and Wendy and Bill didn't want to give up what they feel is an important part of their daughter's life. Wendy talked to two other women whose children attended Shannon's preschool class, and now they each provide two-way transportation one day a week.

Chicken Pox and Tummyaches

A sick child can be hazardous to your employment. When mothers are the only ones who stay home to care for an ill child, employers may be less than patient. If both parents share the care, job stress is eased.

Most employers offer a specified number of personal leave days. But childhood illnesses can quickly use up that allotment without even counting the time needed for routine doctor's appointments and school conferences. When both parents take turns staying home with a sick child, or for their special appointments, you can arrange needed time-off around job schedules more easily.

My daughter must arrive at work in time to open her employer's office, but her husband has a gardening service and can set his own work hours. When one of their children is ill, Sal stays home mornings while Dana goes to work. In the afternoon when it's easier for Dana to take time off, they trade places. If the weather is bad and Sal can't work, he stays home all day. In exchange for this flexibility the whole family may have to work on the weekend to help Dad catch up on *his* work.

If both you and your husband are locked into tight schedules at work that don't allow for unexpected time off, you will have to make special arrangements for a sick child.

Employers are generally understanding about day care glitches and sick children. But even the most patient employer can't afford to keep someone on the payroll who spends more time away from the job dealing with family problems than they spend on the job working. Unreliable day care and children's illnesses are the top reasons for absenteeism of working mothers.

Find out how much personal leave your employer allows for handling child care emergencies such as illness and disruptions in child care arrangements. Check to see if you can take vacation pay for any time needed in excess of personal leave.

Good communication with your employer before an emergency strikes can make it easier to request time off when it is necessary. Offer to come in early, stay late, or work on a weekend to make up time. See if you can take paperwork home with you. An employer who knows you take your job and your parenting duties seriously will respect and work with you.

Avoiding Morning Madness

The only way to describe mornings in a household where mother works is *chaotic*—not always total chaos, but near enough to qualify for disaster aid. Children don't want to get out of bed, shoes play hide-and-bet-you-can't-find-me, and someone always needs lunch money or an empty egg carton for art class or three dozen cupcakes for sharing.

To eliminate some of the chaos, start getting ready for morning the evening before. After dinner, and before leaving the table, poll everyone on tomorrow's needs. Keep a pad and pencil handy so you or Dad can make notes. Are there school papers to be signed and returned to school? Does anyone need special transportation? Do books need to be returned to the library? Who needs something washed, ironed, or mended? A written list allows you to check off items in preparation for morning.

Assign tasks before dispersing for the evening. While one parent or an older child clears the dinner table, the other parent can supervise tomorrow's readiness.

By starting right after dinner, there is still time for Dad to do an extra load of laundry while you bake that batch of forgotten cupcakes. If your schedule allows it, you may even start your planning before dinner.

A master calendar plus an accessible bulletin board (or refrigerator with magnets) is great for overall planning. Enter appointments, school and church events, and memos as soon as you get them, and refer to the calendar each evening to stay on top of your busy lives.

Bagging It

Knowing what you and the kids are going to wear the next day will eliminate one of morning's biggest hassels.

All but the very youngest child can lay out clothes for the next day. If children have difficulty matching clothes, make up clothing packets when you fold clean laundry. Combine complete outfits and put them into drawers or closets.

Use plastic grocery bags with handles to keep everything together. Boys' shirts and jeans can be folded and slipped into plastic bags along with underwear and matching socks. Girls' outfits can be hung together on one hanger with plastic bags attached to hold hair ribbons, barrettes, or other accessories.

Each child should have a duffle bag for school permission papers, homework assignments, and any items that must go to school or to day care. Dad's briefcase and Mom's shoulderbag help keep parents organized, too. Post-it notes reminding kids or adults of special duties can be stuck to their bags. Then put everyone's carryall where they won't be forgotten in the morning rush.

An old-fashioned hall tree is wonderful for keeping coats, galoshes, and school bags together. If you don't have a hall tree, put up an expandable mug or coat rack to hang things on, install an extra shelf in the coat closet, or place a bookcase, cabinet, or storage cubes near your main exit door to help you keep organized.

Creating calm out of chaos isn't easy. But it can be done if the whole family works together. Put on your thinking cap when problems arise and pray for inspiration. You'll be surprised what you can come up with!

6

Just a Little More Time

How to Make the Minutes Count

What do working mothers have the least and need the most? *Time!*

It's all too easy to become so busy working that we neglect husband, children, church, and self. We often look for time and say we can't find it. In reality we have the time, we just may not be optimizing our use of it. We hear so much about "quality" time, but quality time is every minute of every day.

Plan and budget your time as you do your family finances. By making every minute count, you can stop looking wistfully for big chunks of time. Like bonus checks, they seldom come and never when you really need them!

Precious Moments

Working mothers need lots of spiritual nourishment. God can only feed you when you spend time with Him and in His Word.

Start and end each day with prayer. Somehow a day that begins with prayer seems to go smoother. Those precious minutes with God seem to multiply like the loaves and fishes to give us the time to do what needs to be done.

Get up early; stay up late. Turn the television off half an hour before bedtime to prepare for family devotions.

Play worship tapes in your car or tune into an inspirational radio station on your drive to work. Hymns of praise are soothing when you're tired, and special messages can direct your thoughts along positive paths all day long. If you walk or take public transportation, buy an inexpensive tape player with ear phones.

Don't neglect regular church attendance and, if possible, keep active in one area of Christian service that you enjoy. Although you may want to make some changes in how and where you will serve, be faithful once you make a commitment. You may want to work with children to keep you in touch with your own children's interests and activities. Or try a complete change of pace and work with seniors, a visitation ministry, or women's group.

Maintaining Togetherness

Creativity is a must in finding ways to spend time as a couple. It may be easier and quicker to drive to work, but riding the bus with your husband might give you more time to talk without interruption. If you drive together, shut off the radio and give each other your undivided attention—drivers must keep their eyes on the road, however.

Decide how to optimize the use of your time together. Do you want to solve problems? Go over the budget? Make plans? Or just let the thoughts flow? Working people use agendas and meeting guidelines to keep business discussions on target, so consider using the same techniques to get the most from your precious moments alone.

Perhaps you may want to divide the commute into segments—from the day care center to the freeway is for quiet contemplation; the freeway course is for brainstorming and problem solving; and the last stretch to the first person's destination is for each other.

Small periods of time tucked here and there into your days are important, but you also need to spend some larger and more concentrated time together away from the children. Trade off child care with your family members. Invite your niece or nephew for an overnight stay, and ask your brother or sister to return the favor by watching your children. Ask grandparents to give you a weekend of babysitting instead of a birthday or anniversary gift.

Build a support group with neighbors and friends to exchange child care. Perhaps this could be a project for the young married group at your church. Divide into two teams and let one team take all the kiddies for a Friday night sleepover at church while the other couples plan an adults-only outing, a relaxing day together, or a romantic evening. Meet at church to deliver the children back to their own families.

Time alone with each other is necessary to nurture all the wonderful things that made you choose to live together until death do you part! Reaffirm your commitment to one another. Talk to each other and talk to God together. Keep the lines of communication open in all directions.

You need time to discuss your individual and family needs and to evaluate how you're meeting those needs. What about the goals that you set? If they seem to have gotten lost, or are no closer than when you began this two-income lifestyle, you need to redefine your goals or examine your methods of reaching them.

Scheduling in Your Kids

Children perceive time differently than adults. While you may want larger chunks of time to spend with your spouse, children are often satisfied with mini-moments. Their attention span is short, so a few minutes scheduled more frequently can be very satisfying to them.

Infants require a lot of physical care—diapering, bathing, and feeding times can be used as social times, too. It's a shame to do these tasks automatically when you can make them special moments of closeness. Hug, caress, talk, smile, and play with your little one each time you pick him or her up.

Toddlers love to share what is going on in their lives. Take time to listen to them and ask questions so they can feel important. Look at their drawings and admire their towers of blocks.

Older children may need longer periods of attention. Set aside time for them together and as individuals. Take an interest in their school and church activities. Rather than an intimidating or artificial "time to talk," share an interesting activity. Place a large puzzle on a card table in the family room and work on it together. Start a stamp collection, or offer to keep score for their sports team.

You schedule dental appointments and car servicing, why not schedule time for your children? Write it on your calendar just like you do your child's medical check up. Work through coffee breaks and pick up your child early and go for milk and cookies at a coffee shop. Let the children take turns staying up late on weekends and plan a special activity just for them.

Children measure your love for them by the undivided attention you give them. The last thing you want your child to think is, Mom's job is more important to her than me. A few moments a day can make a difference for a lifetime.

Half the Time, Twice the Work

Do two things at once. Clean out a kitchen drawer while talking on the phone. Bake a cake while the roast is in the oven. Go over spelling words with your child while folding laundry.

Use your transportation time to good advantage. Play word games, sing songs, or tell riddles while driving to and from child care. Borrow story or book tapes from the library and play them while you drive. You can even record a special message to your loved one and then switch tapes the next day.

Writing letters is an almost forgotten art these days, but you can still write notes or postcards—and you don't have to limit them to those who live far away. A written note is a terrific way to communicate special thoughts. Surprise your husband or children with a letter or note.

Keep a stack of picture or plain postcards in your purse, desk or briefcase, and send a quick message to someone you care about. Congratulate a child on a good grade, a great home run, or just getting home from school on time. Send your husband a love note. Use gummed note pads to hide a surprise message in a pocket, a school book, or lunch bag.

People Priorities

The Bible tells us to put first things first. (See Matthew 6:31-33.) Our spiritual relationships should top any list. Put Christ first in your life and the rest will fall into place. The spiritual strength you receive through church worship and service will help you balance your busy life.

Although God tells us not to worry about food and clothing (dusting, dishes, and dirty laundry), we know that

He does expect us to be responsible in caring for ourselves and our family. Sometimes, however, we forget that people should always come before things.

Don't become so busy in "keeping house" that you forget to have fun. Find ways to get the necessities done so you will have more time for each other. If you make the moments count, you'll be making memories that will last forever.

7

Supermom Doesn't Live Here Anymore

The Care and Nurturing of Working Moms

Husbands may be the head of the household, but women are its heart. The human heart pumps life-giving blood to vital organs to maintain the total body. Women provide the same function for the family body. The loving care of a wife and mother keeps her family alive and vital.

Too often we forget that we, as women, need to nourish ourselves in order to nourish others. Caring for ourselves is usually the first thing we drop from our list of "things to do." How can we possibly fit one more thing into our already super-busy life? Where do we find time for ourselves between child care, housework, cooking, church, work, and being a wife?

There aren't any easy answers. God doesn't give working women extra hours in their days any more than He gives mothers that much-needed extra pair of hands when a baby is born. He does give us His Word to guide us, His promises to encourage us, and His love to lift us.

Working mothers need to follow the scriptural pattern for balanced living found in Psalm 37:3-7. This passage encourages us to trust in the Lord, delight in the Lord, commit our way to the Lord, and "to be still before the Lord." When we follow these instructions—trust, delight, commit, and rest—we will find a way to meet both our needs and our family's needs.

The Martyr Myth

Women are taught to put others first. We are the nurturers, the supporters, and the caregivers. But we have let myths of Supermom, madonnahood, and martyrdom keep us slaves to silly roles and standards that are impossible to achieve. These same myths prevent us from searching out the real source of successful living because they cause us to rely on self rather than on Christ.

Let's do some mental housecleaning and sweep those myths away. You don't have to be a Supermom who can leap piles of unwashed laundry, see through computer terminal tangles, and dash faster than a speeding bullet after a toddler bent on mayhem. Madonnas went out with Michelangelo—can you imagine any female looking saintly without Pampers and permanent press? Martyrs need causes and frankly, I can't think of anything in my life (other than God, husband, and children) worthy of martyrdom.

While women aren't *totally* taken in by these Supermom myths (at least in our saner moments), a part of us still wants to encompass those lofty ideals into our own characters. We want to be efficient, organized, and tireless; we always want to be patient, selfless, and loving. We really don't mind giving up the pair of new, all-purpose leather pumps so the kids can have the latest in designer tennis shoes.

Yet those very qualities, no matter how much we'd like them, aren't always in our family's best interest, especially if we want them in mythical proportions. My mother used to tell us that her imperfections as a parent made us strong! We learn from our mistakes and those of others.

When we try to become Madonnas, perfect mothers, or martyrs who sacrifice ourselves for our family, we are saying we don't trust God. We are telling God, "I'd rather do it myself." God doesn't expect us to be perfect. "Trust in the Lord and do good" (Psalm 37:3). He only wants us to do our best and leave the rest to Him.

Depending on ourselves or the world is like planting seeds in stony places—we will not have strength to endure the trials that come. The one who has no roots, "lasts only a short time. When trouble or persecution comes because of the word, he quickly falls away" (Matthew 13:21).

When we are firmly rooted in the rich soil of faith, our spirits are nurtured so we in turn can nurture others. We can rest in God's promises that He will supply the strength we need to be the best individuals, wives, and mothers—whether we are working on the job or at home. We need only trust in His promises.

The Guilt Trap

While time may be in short supply for working moms, guilt and conflict are available in abundance.

Being a working parent adds more complications to the awesome task of being a mother. We find it almost impossible to do everything ourselves, yet we can't seem to delegate responsibilities because mothers are supposed to be able to do it all. We still feel we are the only ones who should clean, cook, and care for the children. We want help, but we don't ask for it. We get help and have difficulty accepting it.

We feel guilty if we aren't there for every special moment in our infant's life. We feel guilty if dinners are late or the laundry doesn't get folded. We are torn between staying home with an ill child and not getting the financial report ready for the boss's important sales meeting.

We agonize over getting home late and feeding the family leftovers or pizza for the second time in a week. We worry and wonder if we're being good wives, good mothers, and good employees.

We forget that stay-at-home mothers have problems, too. Baby could just as well smile for the first time while Mom is taking out the trash. Dinners can be late because you got tied up at the pediatrician's; laundry doesn't get folded because your mother-in-law stopped by for the morning and stayed the whole day.

We forget the times we left a mildly ill child with a sitter to go out shopping or to a church function. Missing special moments, getting home late, and serving leftovers too frequently can and will happen whether you are working or not!

Somehow the conflict and guilt get blown out of proportion because you are "working." Working isn't a sin—it's just a fact of life that you may or may not be able to choose.

Delighting in the Challenge

Like everything else in life we need to learn to make the best possible choice and then make the best of that choice. What we can't control we can trust to God.

So let's put aside the myths; put aside the conflict and guilt and *delight* in what God has given us. "Delight yourself in the Lord and he shall give you the desires of your heart" (Psalms 37:4).

A job outside the home can bring a valuable insight and understanding to the woman who has never worked before. I learned how difficult it was to deal with the sometimes anti-Christian attitudes in the workplace. I now understand that businessmen use different yardsticks for judging values and making decisions. When you work in the world, you learn things that can help you witness with more wisdom. I feel that I can be a better wife and mother because of my experience working outside the home.

Working gives women tangible rewards that are often lacking in her job at home—paychecks, praise, and promotions. At home sometimes all you get is a hug! If you're blessed in having both on-the-job and at-home rewards, you are indeed fortunate.

Many women like the challenges of the workplace and the exhilaration of competition. Their families flourish and grow from the total experience. The woman who enjoys her job is a happier wife, mother, and individual.

As we delight in the Lord, we can delight in all the wonderful aspects of working. Solving a computer problem on the job is exciting. But so is balancing the responsibilities of work and home. See it as a challenge—a skill to be mastered, a mountain to be climbed.

Take pride in doing a good job at work and at home. Both are important, and women who do both well deserve respect. Cherish the friends you make at the workplace and appreciate the knowledge you gain.

Use what you learn about yourself in the work world to help you at home and vice versa. Organizing a household or an office isn't that different. "And whatever you do, whether in word or deed, do it all in the name of the Lord Jesus, giving thanks to God the Father through him" (Colossians 3:17).

Commit whatever you do to the Lord. Make a commitment to your husband, your family, and your job—in that order! There really is joy in serving others when you are in God's will. Delighting in knowing that all is well when

God is Lord over your life will make that commitment a service rather than a burden.

"Commit your way to the Lord; trust in him and he will do this: He will make your righteousness shine like the dawn, the justice of your cause like the noonday sun" (Psalms 37:5-6).

Special Treats

"I would like one day to do absolutely nothing."

"I would like someone to fix me a cup of tea when I come home tired."

"I'd like to read the newspaper without interruption."

Sound familiar? Working women don't ask for expensive gifts. They don't expect to have full-time cleaning ladies. What they do want is thoughtfulness. The next time your husband, children, or other family and friends ask you what you want for a gift, present them with a list of the things that would make you happiest.

You might want to add these to the things listed above:

—To have hubby balance the check book
—A manicure—better yet—a pedicure with foot massage
—A leisurely bubble bath
—Two hours shopping without the children
—Three hours to clean house without family underfoot
—A long walk to nowhere
—Help with, or better yet someone to completely do, Christmas shopping and/or Christmas cards

Add to your personal list of "treats" anything that would give you a lift. Maybe your husband can take over grocery shopping—permanently! Someone could do the household task you hate the most—even if it's just once. Have your windows washed, oven cleaned, or the dog groomed rather than doing it yourself. Ask for a book of coupons for the car wash for your birthday.

What about the gift of a listening ear? How many times have you listened to your husband complain about his job? Does he listen as attentively to your work problems? Women need to let off steam about job frustration, too. Let your husband know that you need equal time in this department.

Consider setting aside the second fifteen minutes at home (the first fifteen minutes is for family) to talk with your husband. Make a pot of coffee, get the children started on homework, or settle them in front of a good video tape, and spend time just clearing away the workday problems. Then put them aside and concentrate on a pleasant evening with family.

The list of special treats is endless, and it can be fun to think up ways to treat yourself to a physical and mental rest from all your responsibilities. Here's one from Psalm 37 that you may not have considered: "Be still before the Lord and wait patiently for him" (verse 7).

Resting (being still) in God's promises helps us to be patient in how He works out the details of our lives. Physical relaxation gives us that day to day patience to wait on God's will for us. We need to nurture ourselves with spiritual and physical rest to have the energy we need to be working women with families.

[illegible]

[illegible] happiness momentarily. They must be [illegible] special, loving care.

8

The Only Parent

Special Needs of the Single Working Mother

Single mothers generally don't have a choice whether or not to work. They carry the full load of earning a living, parenting the children, and making ends meet on a limited income.

Whether you're widowed, divorced, or never-married, the problems remain the same—too little money, not enough time, and no energy. Because of your unique situation as a single working mother, you have special needs.

Raising a family alone is difficult. Single parents must be aware of their children's needs, but they should also attend to their own needs. You can't take care of your children unless you take care of yourself first.

Nurturing Family Ties

As a the single working mother, you need a strong support system. It's important to cultivate relationships with your natural family and your church family to build a network of caring, concerned people. But such relationships do not happen automatically. They must be nurtured with tender, loving care.

With family you can be yourself without any explanations. They know and love you. They also understand that you may need extra help and attention now, but that it wasn't and won't always be that way. Enjoy your special place in the family and let them know when you need help.

Parents may want to help but may not know how. They may be overprotective or seemingly uncaring because they don't know what you need. You can ease the awkwardness of the situation by communicating your needs and how they can help.

Do you need advice? Financial help? Do you just need to know that they love you no matter what mistakes you've made or how you're handling your life? Be patient with your family and yourself as you all learn to cope with single parenthood.

There's a tendency, in mothers of grown children especially, to want to re-parent a child after a marital breakup. When my daughter's marriage ended, I wanted to share all the things I didn't tell her the first time around, hoping I could protect her from getting hurt again.

I finally realized that I couldn't live her life for her—she had to make her own decisions in her own way. I had to learn to trust her to do the best she could under difficult circumstances. Today I'm very proud of her. She's overcome tremendous obstacles, and I often wonder if I could have done as well.

My daughter learned we loved her no matter what and that we really did want to help her. She also learned that she had to tell me occasionally, "I love you, Mama, but I have to do it myself." We both grew through the experience because we loved each other enough to listen.

Faithful Support

Divorced Christians are often overwhelmed by a sense of spiritual failure. Divorce seems to be a visible "sin" that stains their self-image and separates them from the fellowship they need now more than ever. Widows may find more support from others, but even that dwindles long before she may feel ready to handle life alone.

All the support in the world doesn't change the fact that you are responsible for the majority of what happens in your life. You have to make the decisions, big and small. You have to accept the responsibility for the consequences of those decisions.

Your Christian brothers and sisters can become like second family. Now is the time to become more active, not less active, at church. You need a strong spiritual grounding more than ever.

You may not be able to attend all the services, but make Sunday worship an unfailing habit. Your children need to see you standing faithfully before the Lord. They need your example of church attendance, prayer, and faith to teach them that God does indeed meet all their needs.

Don't stop at just church attendance. Get involved and become a vital part of the church family. Choose at least one other activity that you can enjoy—choir, teaching or helping in Sunday school, serving on a committee, or working on the church bulletin. Take your children to Sunday school and youth group meetings. Contact with Christian men and fathers at church can meet a special need in the lives of children being raised by a woman.

Your Special Ministry

If your church doesn't have a single parents' group, you may want to make that your special ministry. Single parents often feel dreadfully alone in a church setting of twosomes. An informal group that meets for coffee after evening services or takes turn hosting a social can be fun and inspiring. Sharing your experiences, problems, and solutions will foster growth in all of you.

Don't feel that you only fit in with singles, though. Older families at church can be wonderfully supportive. The seniors are especially loving and caring. If your children are very young, working with a teen group will give you insight into what's ahead with your own family.

You need the kind of positive, godly support that Christian fellowship can provide. It's too easy for singles to get caught up in a worldly lifestyle because of loneliness or depression. Don't let that happen to you. Your children need the firm foundation of a Christian home. And that's something you can give them with or without a husband.

One of my favorite verses is Proverbs 3:5,6—"Trust in the Lord with all your heart and lean not on your own understanding; in all your ways acknowledge him, and he will make your paths straight."

As a single parent, you may feel you have no one to turn to. Yet when you know Christ as your Savior, you are never alone. No matter how your singleness came about, you need to remember that God loves you. Trust in Him, read His Word for direction, and then trust in Him again to see you through whatever happens.

You and Your Children

Your children need you, and you need them. Together, with the Lord's help, you can overcome anything.

Some children may feel the stigma of single-parent status more strongly than others. You can ease the pain of being daddyless by helping your child understand why you are living apart. I grew up in a single-parent family, but I never felt deprived because I knew both my parents loved me.

If your ex-spouse is available, keep communication open so you can work together for your child's sake. When a father is totally out of the picture, however, you need to reassure your child that Daddy's absence has nothing to do with him or her.

As your children mature, you will want to share your problems with them. You don't have go into detail about your finances, worries, or plans, but it is important to be honest with them about your situation.

Focus on the things you do have. Remind your children and yourself of God's perfect love no matter what your circumstances. The apostle Paul said, "I have learned to be content whatever the circumstances" (Philippians 4:11).

Believe that God can take what is happening in your lives at this time and use it for your good. Search His Word for the help He has to offer, the comfort that is readily available, and the reassurance that He is always with you.

Work as a family to make the most of your own situation. Let your children know that you value their opinions and need their help. Children often have insight and solutions that adults haven't considered. Don't focus only on the now, but on the past and the future—and their relationship to each other in God's plan.

Children love to hear stories about their past. Spend an evening reading their baby books, looking at photograph albums, and telling them stories about your family, their father's family, and themselves.

Talk about now. How do they feel about what's going on in your lives? What would they like to change? Why? Take time to enjoy where you are right now. Savor the simple things like making popcorn, taking a walk, or participating in church activities.

Take lots of photos to record your lives. Let the children take pictures of you so they won't have a photo album minus Daddy *and* Mommy. If they aren't old enough to use a camera, make sure a friend takes an occasional shot of you alone and with the kids.

Plan the future. When children feel part of planning, they are less fearful. Let them know that problems are temporary and life can change. If you don't know what is going to happen next year, talk about next month, next week—even tomorrow. Plan to enjoy the journey into the future together.

Stretch Yourself, Not the Budget

As much as you love the children, you need time for yourself, too. Don't make the children your only focus in life because one day they will grow up and leave home. You need to nurture yourself so when they do leave, you aren't left lonely as well as alone.

Take time for a hobby as simple as needlepoint or as complicated as computers. Take a class one night a week. You need adult company, and you could learn new skills to improve your financial situation. Sign up for exercise or dance classes. There are many community and adult education classes that are free or inexpensive. Join a social organization or church group that focuses on adult activities. Whatever you choose, make sure it is something you enjoy. If you build skills, improve yourself, or make new friends, that's a bonus.

If you're having trouble making ends meet, consider retraining into a more lucrative field. An excellent program for single mothers is the federal Job Training and Placement Act with funds administered by state social services. JTPA provides job training and placement for low-income and welfare recipients. The program pays for transportation to and from training and they even pay for child care in some specially funded programs.

In addition, some non-profit organizations offer scholarships for women who are furthering their education. Contact your local chapters of the American Business Woman Association, Soroptomist, League of Women Voters, and American Association of University Women for details. Soroptomists gives an amount that may be spent in any way the recipient chooses rather than just on education. These organizations also provide good emotional support and networking to help you improve your job opportunities.

Find out about government-funded programs to aid single mothers and working parents in low-income jobs. A new program in our area is even finding low-cost housing for job trainees or those who are in programs to further their education.

Family and child social service agencies administer funds for everything from free dairy products for women and children to subsidized child care and food stamps. Asking for assistance is hard. But when you ask for help to help yourself, you will reach total independence sooner.

Grow in Giving

You don't always have to be on the receiving end of others' good deeds. "Give, and it will be given to you. A good measure, pressed down, shaken together and running over, will be poured into your lap. For with the measure you use, it will be measured to you" (Luke 6:38).

Blessings are even more blessed when they are returned and passed on. My mother bought a broom for a young bride who didn't have one. Twenty years later that woman bought another needy newlywed, me, an egg beater. Those small gifts given in love were precious because they symbolized the importance of passing on the help that was received in a time of need.

As a single parent, you need to grow in giving, especially if you are frequently the recipient of others' generosity. Look for ways you can return or pass on favors. Even the neediest can give gifts of time and companionship.

Run errands for your babysitter on your lunch hour; do your mom's hand mending while you watch TV in the evening; offer your home for the youth group's singspiration; or share a casserole with the senior citizen who pitched in to watch your child when he had chicken pox and you couldn't take off work.

The Best Things in Life Are (Almost) Free

You can't afford not to take the time for yourself. If the budget is squeezed to the point that there really isn't any money left for you, then look for activities that don't cost anything.

A walk in the park is free. Let the kids play while you read a book under a tree. Take a picnic lunch with you and make a day of it.

Meeting a friend for window shopping is free. Trade babysitting with another mother who needs time to herself.

Work through your breaks and take a shorter lunch hour to cut time off your work day, and then use it for yourself. Stop off for coffee, take a walk, or go home and soak in a bathtub of bubbles before picking up the children. You'll feel refreshed and better able to cope with re-entry into the madness of single parenthood.

My mother raised us alone. She worked as a telephone operator in the days before direct dialing, and the constant sound of voices in her ear all day was extremely stressful. Her job made it even more difficult to come home to four very vocal little people. The minute she walked in the door we hit her with all our problems. "Marsh didn't feed the dog!" "Timmy hit me." "Beth can't boss me around; I can take care of myself." "Carolyn came home from school late."

My mother didn't have any extra money, much less time, for herself. She didn't even have her own bedroom to retreat to. But Mama found a way to cope. Each night when she came home from work, she went straight from the front door to the bathroom, newspaper in hand, and stayed there until she'd read it from cover to cover. Nothing less than bloodshed kept her from that twenty minutes alone.

Mama was also big on picnics and visits to her sister's farm where she could turn us all loose amid the cows and blackberry bushes and ignore us for a few hours. We loved it!

It isn't easy—but it is possible to find time for yourself, and it will help you keep your sanity until things get better.

Single—But Not Alone

Single parents don't need anyone to tell them their lives aren't easy—they live it day by day. You do need the assurance that God understands you and has not forsaken you.

You can probably identify with the words of the apostle Paul: "We are hard pressed on every side, but not crushed; perplexed, but not in despair; persecuted, but not abandoned; struck down, but not destroyed. . . . For our light and momentary troubles are achieving for us an eternal glory that far outweighs them all. So we fix our eyes not on what is seen, but on what is unseen. For what is seen is temporary, but what is unseen is eternal" (2 Corinthians 4:8, 9, 17, 18).

Keep your eyes on Jesus and on the eternal rewards of living according to His Word, and you will have the peace that passes understanding.

You may be single, but you certainly aren't alone.

Part Two

Finding, Evaluating, and Keeping Quality Day Care

9

Who Will Watch My Children?

Solving the Day Care Crisis

Children are a heritage from the Lord—precious treasures that bring with them abundant joy and some pretty heavy responsibilities. But with more women than ever before having to work outside the home, some of that responsibility is by necessity being delegated to caregivers outside the family circle.

"I can't wait until I finish my master's degree and get a job," said Judy, Marcy and Derek's mother, as she chatted with her children's licensed day care provider. "I'm really looking forward to working again."

Judy is a typical contemporary woman. She married in college, worked for awhile, and then quit to have her children. During the past year she returned to school full time to prepare for re-entry into the work world.

While her current caregiver has been able to fit Marcy and Derek into her group of day care charges, she hasn't told Judy yet that she doesn't have any full-time openings for them. Maybe, she hopes, by the time Judy finds a job she will.

Unavailable or Unreliable

As more mothers like Judy go to work, the nation's child care facilities are hard pressed to meet the growing need. The National Commission on Working Women states that 9.3 million children from birth to five years of age and a total of 24 million children age thirteen years and younger received child care while parents worked.

A conservative estimate of "latchkey" children—children who care for themselves and/or siblings for at least part of the day—is seven million under the age of thirteen. Child care services have not kept pace with demand. Children needing care simply outnumber the available child care spaces.

Judy planned to re-enter the work world when her children were older since before and after-school care isn't as difficult to find as infant care. Many elementary schools are now starting on-site after-school child care programs. If care isn't available, Judy is fortunate that she has the option to stay home for a while longer.

The mother who can choose when and whether to return to work faces a wider selection of child care alternatives. Women who don't have a choice find less child care options available, which compounds an already difficult situation.

Nancy is a divorced mother of two pre-schoolers. "I have to work, but finding someone to watch the kids has been hard. At first I tried babysitters. When they were unreliable, I found a center I liked. But it wasn't conveniently located, and it was expensive. This past year I've had six sitters. I know the children need more stability, but I can't find anyone on a permanent basis.

"Everyone wants to babysit," Nancy continued, "until it conflicts with other things they want to do. They seldom give any notice, and many times I've taken the children to the sitter in the morning to find out she's quit. My boss has been understanding about my child care problems, but his patience is wearing thin."

Searching for a Sitter

Kathy has three children—four months, six and eight years old. She works partly from financial need, but mainly because she enjoys it. "I've worked since I got out of school," she said. "I did stay home six months one time, but after so many years of working I couldn't adjust to being a full-time homemaker. And the entire family likes the higher standard of living that an extra paycheck gives us."

Child care has been a problem for Kathy, too. "I had the same sitter for five years. Then we moved into a new home in another part of town. Because the kids wanted to go to school with their new neighborhood friends, I decided to change sitters. My husband was able to see the kids off to school, so I hired a college student to come in at noon when Jonathan got out of kindergarten. That worked until I found out she wasn't always there when he got home. One day he sat on the doorstep for almost an hour waiting for her.

"Then the kids complained that the sitter dragged them all over while she did errands, visited with friends or went to the laundromat. I wanted the children to be able to play with their school chums, but they never got a chance."

When Kathy got pregnant with her third child, she decided to make another change. She took two months maternity leave and spent it trying to find child care. Because of the new baby, her first choice was someone to come into her home. She advertised in the local paper for two weeks, but the response was disappointing.

"Only four people called and two of those weren't interested enough to come for an interview. Of the two who came for interviews, one was a teenage dropout who was only interested in the TV—was it color, and did we have cable service? The second was an older woman who was more concerned about keeping the kids quiet and the house immaculate than she was in nurturing them. Neither even asked to see the baby."

Kathy then looked for someone who would babysit in their own home. She talked to neighbors and friends, called the school secretary and the day care licensing department, and watched newspaper ads. But few people would take three children and most didn't want an infant.

Kathy finally found a neighbor who agreed to fill in temporarily. "I know Dorothy doesn't want to babysit, but even if it is only for a few months, it will give me time to find someone permanent."

Nancy and Kathy learned firsthand about the child care crises. Perhaps Judy will have an easier time finding care for her two children when she returns to work. Finding child care is one of the biggest problems working mothers face. Not everyone has the difficulties that Nancy and Kathy had, but their problems are typical.

Any kind of child care is often hard to find. *Quality* child care that meets all your needs may not be available at any cost. And those who need child care the most are generally hit the hardest by shortages of available, affordable care.

Now the Good News

If the day care picture sounds grim, it is. But the good news is that it is getting brighter as more people are seeing the need and finding ways to meet it. Communities, schools, and organizations are studying the child care crisis to find solutions. Businesses are discovering that providing child care, child care referrals, counseling and/or benefits are cost-effective when weighed against absenteeism due to unreliable child care.

Parents, especially Christian parents who are committed to parenting in the deepest sense, are creating and developing resources where none existed. Finding child care may be difficult, but it isn't impossible.

When the woman who babysat for her two youngest children decided to get out of the child care business, Ginny was left to find a replacement. Fortunately, as a teacher, she had the summer to look. Her daughter was still an infant, and Ginny was very particular about the kind of care she received. After advertising and interviews proved fruitless, she went to prayer.

She told the Lord she needed a Christian woman who didn't smoke and who lived close to the school or bus stop. Two days before school started, a neighbor told Ginny about Marge. A committed Christian who considered caring for children as her ministry, Marge proved to be the answer to Ginny's prayers—over and above what she had asked. Marge's care for the children has extended beyond their physical needs to nurturing them spiritually and emotionally.

A contemporary, Christian working woman who wants to "watch over the affairs of her household" (see Proverbs 31:27) must arrange for a mother-substitute while she fulfills her duties outside the home. Finding any child care isn't easy, but finding quality care that supports and enhances our spiritual responsibilities as parents takes a little more time and effort and a lot of prayer!

10

What's Available

Your Shopping Guide to Child Care

While the demand for child care is still greater than the resources available, that very need has created more child care options than ever before.

Generally, child care falls into three categories:

1. Home care—care in your home
2. Family day care—care in the home of the caregiver
3. Child care centers

A fourth category includes miscellaneous care such as latchkey programs, self-care, and combinations of different types of care.

Home Care

Home care is generally the most expensive child care unless you are blessed with a doting grandmother who works cheap. Today with many grandmothers in the work force, great-grandmothers may be more readily available. Other relatives are also a good source of caregivers to come into your home since they may be more inclined to work for a nominal fee.

If a family member isn't available, senior citizens or college students can be hired. There are also agencies specializing in providing "nannies" for hire.

Household tasks are sometimes included with home care, but these are usually limited to the child's needs such as meal preparation and perhaps light housekeeping and some laundry. If you need more than general housekeeping, be specific about what you want and be prepared to pay more for a combination caregiver-housekeeper. It may be to your advantage to hire one person for child care and another for housekeeping.

Home care is especially good for very young children, infants, families with several children, and for mothers who work unusual hours. Social Security must be paid by you as the "employer" for workers who come to your home on a regular basis.

Family Day Care

Family day care that provides care in the home of the caregiver is divided into two sub-categories: *licensed* and *unlicensed.*

Each state decides if and how to regulate home child care. Some states exempt caregivers who are caring for a limited number of children and/or caregivers who care for family members. States also differ on whether they require licensing or registration. Call your local child welfare or social service agency for information on state and local regulations.

For the sake of clarity, we will use the terms "provider" or "caregiver" for regulated (licensed or registered) day care and "babysitter" for those who are not regulated.

Both kinds of family day care are less expensive than home care and centers. Family day care rates for additional children are generally less than day care center fees for siblings. While centers may offer a five to ten percent discount for a second child, family day care may discount up to thirty or forty percent.

Like in-home care, family day care is good for infants, younger children, families with more than one child, and mothers with unusual work hours.

The quality of licensed family day care varies widely from home to home. Regulation often deals with only health and safety, not quality. Fingerprinting of all adult members of the household and tuberculin testing of day care providers and their families may be required. Some states do in-depth personal screening that determines a prospective caregiver's suitability for child care. Other states hold group orientation meetings to explain child care ordinances.

Home visits are initially made to check for properly fenced play areas, sanitation, and safety. After approval, home visits may then be repeated during the first year, at renewal of a caregiver's credentials. Inspection may take place randomly on all or a percentage of homes, or when a complaint is made against a home or caregiver. Providers are given prior notice of home visits except in unusual circumstances. Parents are the best judges of child care since they are able to monitor the homes on a daily basis.

Babysitters bypass regulation by simply setting up business without official sanction. Some are not aware of regulatory requirements; others may know about regulations but do not apply for licenses or certification because of the red tape involved.

Regulation does not guarantee quality care nor does lack of official regulation mean inferior care. Most often the provider determines the quality of care that children receive. Regulation is just a starting point. Parents need to begin there and make their own inquiries to insure a day care home is all that it should be.

Care in private homes is as individual as is care within families. Caregivers may be "grandmotherly," creative, energetic, organized, or casual. Some day care homes are operated like mini-preschools with structured play time, outings, and activities. Others are run very casually with lots of caring but few organized activities. The importance of evaluating your needs and expectations and then finding a provider who shares your views cannot be underestimated in achieving a successful day care relationship.

Child Care Centers

Child care centers may be operated by private profit-making, private non-profit, public, church, community, or business organizations. As with family day care, quality is not indicated by type but by the individuals providing the care.

Centers offer a variety of programs, activities, and—perhaps even more important—stability. Because child care of any kind is not particularly well-paying, child care providers, from in-home nannies to day care providers, change jobs frequently. Workers in centers also may change with regularity, but the familiarity of remaining staff, other children, and surroundings make the changes less disruptive for youngsters.

Day care centers are often located centrally or close to public transportation or thoroughfares. Hours of service meet the needs of most working parents on a standard daylight schedule.

Centers may care for infants through preschool or two years of age through early elementary school. Those who take school-aged children may provide transportation to the nearest elementary school. Some private or church schools provide before and after school care on the premises. Few centers, however, care for all age groups from infant through grade school. The majority of centers stop at about the third grade unless they operate a latchkey program.

Cost for centers is lower than in-home care and more expensive than family day care unless you qualify for subsidized assistance. Non-profit centers have a ratio of full-payment and subsidized clients whose full or partial payment is made by government funds. These payments are administered by agencies and based on a sliding scale according to family income. Private and church centers also may have sliding scale rates, and if they don't, often they can refer parents to agencies who administer subsidies.

Some churches now have preschool programs, and those with on-site elementary schools often have before and after school child care. Full-time care, however, is generally not available in churches. If your children are school-aged and there is a good church-operated school in your area that offers child care for students, check it out.

Miscellaneous Care

Latchkey care used to mean that a child was on his own for short periods before and after school while parents worked. Today *latchkey* more often refers to before and after school care provided by child care agencies, schools, or other organizations.

The YMCA was one of the first organizations to institute latchkey programs. Fred Stickney, president of the YMCA of Alameda County, Oakland, California has written a book on developing latchkey programs. Many school districts are renting out unused classrooms for latchkey programs operated by YMCAs or other organizations. Some school districts are starting their own latchkey programs.

Some programs operate during school sessions only, and others continue throughout the summer and on holidays. Latchkey programs provide help with homework, recreational activities, and after school snacks. They are ideal for the older school-aged child who is too young to stay alone and too old for the traditional babysitter.

Self-care. Children caring for themselves before and after school and for longer periods is an option most parents would prefer not to use. But care for school-aged children isn't always easy to find. Older children often do not want to stay with a "babysitter." Parents may opt to let them try it on their own when other care isn't available. Check with local child welfare agencies and police departments for regulations regarding children staying alone.

Combination care. Finding that no one type of care will meet their particular child care needs, some parents may have to combine different kinds of care for their children. Combined care is expensive and time consuming. Just the logistics of getting children to and from different child care and school sites can be awesome. But if combining your child care alternatives means each child will enjoy a safe and nurturing environment, it is worth the effort.

11

Child Care on a Budget

Calculating Costs and Pinching Pennies

No one likes to put a dollar value on child care. If we had our way, teachers, caregivers, and yes, even mothers, would be paid their weight, and then some, in gold. Yet few mothers could afford to pay what quality child care is worth.

If you are going to work to help your family financially, child care costs are an important part of your budget. Phone calls to a sampling of centers and caregivers will give you an idea of the going rates in your community. Add your travel, lunch, and wardrobe costs to the child care figures and subtract this total from your projected income.

Most working mothers find that the cost of family meals is higher when they work because they don't have the time to prepare budget meals. You might spend more on household services than when you were home. Adjust family budget items to reflect this convenience-over-cost practicality. If your net profit after paying out work expenses and child care costs is marginal, you might reconsider your decision to work.

If you don't have any choice but to work, start paring the figures down to more manageable numbers. Use public transportation or a carpool, pack your lunch, and plan to limit spending for high-cost conveniences such as dinners out and household help.

If the Price is Right

With your estimated budget in hand, look at the day care options in chapter ten and weed out those that don't meet your needs for reasons other than cost and those that are definitely out of your price range.

For example, child care in your home can be two to three times more expensive than care in the caregiver's home. If you need home care, explore different ways to make it affordable. Family members, friends, seniors citizens, or college students may charge less than someone from an agency. Offer free room and board to an older person or a college student in exchange for child care. Explore other possible options—perhaps hiring a caregiver in their home would work just as well.

Even within a category, costs may vary. Don't stop with calling one family day care provider, one babysitter, and one center. Call several. Ask about flat fees versus reduced fees if you provide your child's food or disposable diapers.

Ask if you can exchange services for child care. Perhaps you could do a center's bookkeeping in exchange for free child care or a reduced rate, or you might be able to exchange janitorial or gardening services for child care.

Professional caregivers and centers will have information on subsidies that you might qualify for. Many centers base fees on a sliding scale according to your income.

Naturally you will want to pay an affordable fee for child care, but don't let cost be your only guideline for choosing a place for your child. One babysitter may be offering lower rates because she is making up for it by caring for more children. But you probably would be better off paying a higher fee to a caregiver who is caring for fewer children so your child will get more individual attention.

Dependable Day Care

A day care center may be the best choice for the single parent or the working wife who needs absolutely dependable child care. A center doesn't rely on just one caregiver to keep operating. If one staff person decides to quit, or needs time off, the other caregivers keep the system working.

If you choose an individual caregiver, get references so you can check with previous clients to see if the caregiver is reliable. Women who think babysitting sounds easy may give it a try and then quit without notice when they discover it isn't.

Try to find an established sitter or family day care provider who has a proven record for reliability. If a babysitter or day care parent is just starting out and meets all your needs but doesn't have references, be sure to emphasize that you will be depending on her to be there everyday barring an emergency.

"I really didn't want the children in a day care center," said one single parent. "But I had four babysitters in two months. They all loved the children, but the first time they didn't feel like working or something more interesting came along, they quit. I even had another single parent move in to watch the children in exchange for free room and board. Nothing worked, and generally my sitters quit without notice. One time I found out at seven-thirty in the morning that my sitter didn't want to work any more. I had to be at work by eight o'clock! That was the last straw—I found a day care center."

Single parents and working wives with few options don't have the time or energy to constantly be looking for new child care. Reliability must take precedence over convenience and sometimes even cost.

Pinch Hitters

If you are a single parent or a working wife whose husband is unable to assist you with child care, you may have to be more creative about alternatives—especially when you can't afford substitute care during certain times of the year.

Most child care facilities close on only the standard holidays, so that shouldn't interfere with your own work schedule. Occasionally, there is a teachers' work day or an odd day attached to a standard holiday for which you'll have to find alternative care. These days are announced well in advance so you can make other plans.

Again, you might call on family, friends, and neighbors. Another alternative for day care holidays are church young people who are home from college during school breaks. You might even work out a barter system that is mutually beneficial. In exchange for a week of child care, you could send home-baked goodies once a month throughout the year; or sew, mend, and alter college wardrobes; or type term papers.

Your church's youth group might even want to take your children on as a project. Talk to those young people who are studying Christian education and early childhood development and ask if they'd like a little "hands on" experience in the field!

Year-Round Mini-Vacations

When those alternatives don't work out, consider taking your vacation time in small portions throughout the year. Take one week's vacation at Christmas and the second at Easter or Thanksgiving rather than a two-week vacation during the summer. Or take vacations a day or two at a time—an extra day before or after a holiday will give you more time together.

A short vacation during school-year holidays can save you *money*. Most centers and some day care providers charge for standard holidays such as Christmas, New Year's Day, and Thanksgiving. You will be paying double child care fees if you have to pay for substitute care during these times.

If you have time off from work during child care shutdowns for holidays, you can save even more money by creating inexpensive mini-vacations. The children are already excited about the holiday itself, so you need only schedule a few special treats to make a delightful break from your regular routine.

Libraries and recreation departments in most communities schedule free activities for children during school holidays and summer vacations. Our library has an Easter egg hunt and Christmas craft classes plus a summer children's film festival in addition to regular story hours. One library has even scheduled early evening story times for children of working mothers.

Schedule trips to museums, parks, and friends' homes that you don't have time to visit the rest of the year. Spend time baking Christmas cookies or just cleaning, decorating, and rearranging the children's rooms.

Day Care Dollars and Sense

Once you find child care that meets your needs, you've got to figure out how to pay for it. Ask about discounts or sliding fees when choosing child care. If your sitter or center doesn't have special rates, they will probably know where you can get information about subsidies or aid. If they don't have the information you need, look in the yellow pages of your phone book for family support services and child welfare agencies.

Don't be too proud to let your caregiver know when you're having a problem meeting your expenses. Sitters may accept lower rates if they know you are struggling. Centers and sitters may set up easier payment plans, help you get aid, or work out a barter system to offset the cost.

Family day care providers can be a valuable support system for you. My daughter's sitter kept her son supplied in like-new hand-me-downs, bought him shoes, and had her husband cut his hair!

"Sharon was always there when I needed her," said Dana, a working single parent of three. "She even gave me a free week of child care when my subsidy was stopped temporarily. Benjamin is now in school full time, and he still asks to go see Sharon. She is like family to us. Because she is a Christian, Benjamin got excellent care and I know she prayed for him and for all of us."

Preventing Day Care Disasters

Chapter seventeen has general information about backup care to cover holidays and emergencies. Single parents especially need to make doubly sure that they and their caregiver understand how to handle any scheduled or unscheduled lapse in child care services. Ask your provider if they have a substitute for themselves when they need time off for any reason. They may have someone to fill in, or you may need to provide your own back-up.

Ask whether they will care for a sick child. Will they care for an ill child anytime or only under certain circumstances? What criteria do they use to judge when a child may be accepted for the day?

Most caregivers will take a child with a cold, sniffles, or mild tummy ache, but won't take a child with a fever, a child who is vomiting, or one who has diarrhea. When you're using a center or a day care home, caregivers must be cautious about exposing other children in their care to a child in the contagious stages of measles, chicken pox, or strep throat.

Some sitters or centers have an isolation area set up and may take children under some circumstances but not others. Make sure you understand how each situation is handled before your child becomes ill. Ask about back-up care since some sitters have a list of people willing to provide home care for a sick child.

Sick-child care is available for a fee, often a very high fee, in some areas. Local child care agencies should be able to tell you how to contact organizations or individuals who provide such services.

While it is tempting to take a sick child to a caregiver when you know he's ill, please be fair. A sick child may infect other children and perhaps even the caregiver. The entire situation is only made worse when you don't act fairly and responsibly. The little you saved by foisting a sick child on your caregiver is often eaten up if the child takes longer to recuperate or if you lose your sitter's good will by using such tactics.

On the other side of the coin, let your caregiver know that you expect the same fairness in return. Parents should be notified if their children become sick during the day. Unless there is a special isolation area and sanitary precautions are used in caring for a sick child, it isn't fair to the children, parent, or caregiver to expose everyone to a virus or disease.

If the caregiver doesn't provide information or help with sick child care, set up your own back-up system. Find a friend, relative, or neighbor who can fill in for an emergency.

Make Your Child a Blessing

Nobody likes to be backed into a corner—especially at seven thirty in the morning. The best way to offset day care cancellations is to be prepared. Try to obtain firm commitments from reliable friends, family, or neighbors before the unexpected happens.

It is also important not to take advantage of the same people over and over again. If you are courteous and show your appreciation in tangible ways, you can maintain goodwill and not make your child an imposition on somebody else.

Child care on a budget is tricky business, especially if the burden lies mainly on your shoulders. But remember that no problem is too great for God. Pray and ask Him to give you favor with those you need to depend on for child care.

You could also ask the Lord to show you ways to make your children a blessing and not a burden to others. You never know, there might be some lonely grandmother out there just longing for the opportunity to care for a child once in a while.

12

Home Away from Home

Choosing the Right Day Care for You and Your Child

One of the most important things in life is being a parent. When delegating parental responsibilities to others, whether teachers or day care providers, as parents we must remember that we have the final say about our child's care. Our God-given duty is to see that our children are cared for by the best possible person in the best possible environment.

In this chapter we will examine two major factors that must be carefully combined in the optimum day care situation for your family. First, you must consider your child's needs, including his age and personality. Second, you must consider your own needs regarding the availability and convenience of the day care that you are seeking.

Infant, Toddler, or School-Age?

Care in your own home or the home of a caregiver is generally best for very young children from birth to two years. It's easier to have the sitter come to you than hassle with packing up diapers, bottles, and clothing changes for daily trips to a babysitter.

Infants or young children who are prone to colds and other easily-caught illnesses also may do better in their own homes rather than in a center or day care home where they will be exposed to many children.

If home care isn't available, a babysitter or family day care provider is the next best choice. Ask for the number and the ages of the other children who will be in the home. Infants need a lot of individual attention so be sure the caregiver isn't caring for too many children.

Infant care in a center may not be your first choice, but many centers are now setting up specialized infant departments that are quite good. Again, check carefully to be sure your baby will get the individual attention he needs. Because studies show that development and future success at reading and in school depend on these early years, it is especially important that a child get good care during the birth to three-year-old stage.

Toddlers have special needs, too. If this is your toddler's first experience with full-time day care, you may want to choose a small-group situation. Choose a place that is safe for his inquisitive explorations and a caregiver with lots of patience and energy.

Preschoolers need more stimulation and less restrictions than toddlers. Look for a setting with opportunities for learning and growing and a caregiver who challenges young minds.

School-aged children who want to be with their friends may prefer a neighborhood sitter or school-site care program. They need a quiet time to unwind from the pressures of school, a place to do homework, and an understanding person to see them through it all. They want more freedom to explore their environment and an acceptance of their growing sense of independence.

Older children generally don't like going to a "babysitter" because they aren't "babies!" But they aren't quite grown-up, either. Latch-key programs are ideal for them. Staying with their best friend's mother so they can pretend they are just visiting may also work well.

Other choices such as hiring a college student as a companion, trying self-care, and discovering creative child care options are discussed in chapter seventeen, *When All Else Fails.*

One from Column A, Two from Column B

If you have more than one child, look at their age groupings: Are they all preschool, all school-aged, or a combination of ages?

Children who are within an age grouping are easier to place in child care because their needs are similar. Two different groups—infant and toddler; toddler and preschool; or preschool and young school aged may still be placed in one child care setting.

More than two age groups, or children who are widely spaced in age—infant and older child—will probably necessitate a combination of child care. Combination care takes more time to find since you have to suit each child's needs. It is generally more expensive and the commute time between child care sites adds even more to your expense and time budgets.

Family day care or home care may work best for large families both financially and logistically.

Your Child's Personality

Children—even very young children—differ in personality. How does your child relate to other children? Does your child do better in small groups or large ones?

"My daughter was very shy and completely overwhelmed by the child care center I chose for her," said one mother.

"Nicolas was bored at his babysitter's," said another parent. "But when I put him in a center where there were more children to play with and a variety of planned activities, he didn't want to come home at the end of the day!"

Children from Christian families are used to being in nurseries and Sunday school, but that is no guarantee that they will respond well in a new group setting. My son went to the same church from the time he was ten months old, yet until he was eight or nine, he resisted changing classrooms or teachers. He liked the security of sameness. Each change meant a new adjustment.

How does your child respond to adults? Does your little girl get along well with all adults, certain personalities better than others, or does she attach herself to one special person? Some children are very independent and could not care less who is in charge; others need a caregiver who is very responsive and reassuring.

If you have more than one child, each probably has different emotional needs. This may make the search for a day care situation more challenging. It takes time to find just the right place for your child, and even longer when you have more than one child. But taking time to make a right choice the first time is easier on everyone than making a change later.

What Do You Need?

A positive relationship with your child's caregiver is important to your peace of mind. What do *you* need from a caregiver?

Some mothers and caregivers become the best of friends, and the relationship may spill over into their after hours social life. Others become respected allies in providing the best possible care for the child, but they never see each other when the workday is over. A day care relationship generally evolves into a mutually satisfying alliance. But not always.

If you are fortunate to have family to provide child care while you work, you probably already share many ideals and goals on raising children. I never worried when my sister took care of my daughter because we were so much alike. Our ideas on nutrition and discipline were nearly identical. On the other hand, if your mother is caring for your child, she may push sweet snacks when you'd prefer veggie nibbles. Then you are going to have conflicts if you don't agree on some guidelines.

Whether your child is being cared for by a family member, a close friend, a professional caregiver, or at a center, you will have a more satisfying relationship if you feel comfortable with each other. Don't be afraid to ask questions, make suggestions, and candidly discuss your wishes.

If you can't find suitable child care, work with others to promote more and better child care in your area. Perhaps your church has been talking about starting a child care center. The local school might start up a latch-key program if enough parents expressed an interest. You might know of a woman who would be an ideal caregiver if she were approached with the idea of going into business. Later we'll discuss how to create your own child care when none is available.

Convenience Vs. Cost

Convenience is relative. What one mother finds convenient may not be convenient for you. Convenience also may be cost-related. Can you afford convenience? Or is convenience important to you in spite of the cost?

Cost versus convenience isn't always easy to compute. The excellent child care center across town may be expensive, but if it adds miles and hours to your commute time, is it still the best choice for you? The caregiver on the next block may be inexpensive and convenient, but if she doesn't supervise the children and feeds them junk food, is the savings worthwhile?

Convenience may mean better relationships for you or your child. You may choose a center close to home so your children can go to school with their friends. A caregiver close to work may allow you to drop in and have lunch with your child or give you more time to spend together during the commute to work.

Convenience may also mean ease in paying fees. A center may have a fixed pay schedule—all fees due the first of the month. A babysitter, however, may allow you to pay on your regular payday whether it is weekly, bimonthly or monthly.

Convenience may mean flexibility in hours. Centers may operate on a regular daylight, five-day work schedule, but you work swing, graveyard, or weekend shifts. Some latchkey programs close down during summer, which is fine if you have family to provide vacation care or if you can hire a responsible young adult to babysit. But if you can't find reliable summer care, maybe a center or family day care provider who is available year-round would be a better choice.

Finding the Perfect Match

Once you've chosen the kind of day care you think will be best for you and your child, your next step is to find the specific caregiver or center for you. Personal recommendations are usually best. Ask your family, neighbors, church friends, and co-workers about their child care choices.

If you don't get any leads from individuals, look under "babysitters" or "child care" in the business pages of the telephone book. Child care centers, social services that may have referral services, and agencies that provide babysitters should be grouped together.

Some cities have child-care referral agencies that keep current lists of caregivers and centers by neighborhoods. Call the referral agency, give them your address, and they'll send you a print-out or list of caregivers in your area. Pre-schools and nursery schools also may have helpful lists. Not all preschools and nurseries provide all-day care, but some do.

Another good source that many parents overlook is the local elementary school. Unlicensed babysitters and regulated day care providers often leave their names with the school office. This is an especially good source if your child attends the school. If you can't get a caregiver in your child's school district, most school districts will allow a child to attend school where child care is available.

If you work for a large company, ask if they have any child care or child care-related services for employees. Some provide on-site care at the place of employment, either paid entirely or partially by your employer. Other companies offer referral systems where a counselor helps you locate child care.

Leave no stone unturned in your search for day care. Colleges, universities, and senior citizen centers often have job placement offices or at least a bulletin board listing people who are looking for work. Don't forget supermarket bulletin boards and community and business people who are familiar with your neighborhood.

Avon ladies who work suburban neighborhoods know who needs child care and who provides it. Newspapers are perhaps a more current way of looking for child care because caregivers only advertise when they have an opening. You might even decide to run your own ad.

Check it Out

Once you've located a possible child care provider or center, check it out by phone first and then in person. A phone call can gather basic information about rates, hours, licensing, and location. But it can't tell you what the physical or emotional environment is like. Make an appointment to visit the site. If you have the time, it is wise to make two visits—one alone, another with your child.

Child care centers, and in some areas licensed day care homes, are regulated and periodically checked by governmental agencies for the basic health and safety requirements. Babysitters have not met any official regulations.

Before you visit a child care center and/or day care home, call your county social service agency and find out what the regulations are for that particular type of care and ask if the place you are considering is in compliance. Social service or referral agencies often have helpful pamphlets on how to evaluate child care. If they do, ask them to mail you a copy.

If there are no guidelines or checklists available, *A Parent's Guide To Day Care*, published by the U.S. Department of Health and Human Services is excellent. This free government booklet offers a series of checklists on all aspects and areas of child care.

Whether you're using regulated or unregulated care, it is your responsibility to evaluate the suitability of the caregiver and premises for your child. Regulations provide only a starting point. Standards may have relaxed or deteriorated since the last visit by licensing officials. Parents who visit the day care situation everyday are the best judges of care.

Although I encourage mothers to choose regulated care whenever possible, that does not mean that an unlicensed babysitter is not a good caregiver. Most babysitters are excellent.

What You'll Need to Know

Besides the general questions about fees and hours, you will want to know about discipline, meals, and naptimes. How many other children are in care and what are their ages? What kinds of activities are available and how are these supervised?

Make a list of all your questions and refer to it during the interview. If you think of something else after the interview, call again and ask.

Physical facilities should be clean, safe, and comfortable. Check eating areas and bathrooms for cleanliness. Is there proper food storage? Are play areas kept uncluttered for free play? Windows don't have to be spotless—with small children that would be an almost impossible task—but floors where babies crawl should be clean. Outdoor areas should be free of debris. If it is a day care home with pets, animal feces should be disposed of daily.

Safety is important. Check baby furniture, toys, and play equipment for safety and appropriateness. Some older playpens have been declared unsafe because babies' clothing or bodies can get caught. High chairs and cribs should have lead-free finishes. Are toys in good repair and suitable for your child's age and interests? Are tricycles, wagons, and swings well maintained?

Check bathrooms and kitchens to be sure cleaning supplies are properly stored. Family day care homes should have garden chemicals and tools stored safely away from children. Unless there is secure storage for car and garden tools and painting supplies, garages should not be used for play. Outdoors there should be sturdy fences and gates with locks. Of course, a swimming pool should be surrounded by kid-proof fencing and locked gates.

A comfortable environment is one designed for living. If your child is very young, where will he sleep? Is there a play pen available, and if so, how often and why is it used? Playpens are a terrific safety measure when a caregiver has to take another child to the bathroom or is busy fixing lunch, but babies also need freedom to explore their environments.

Space for play, indoors and out, should be adequate for the number and ages of the children in care. Is there a place indoors for quiet play? Is there an area for changing infants? Are toys accessible to toddlers? Do older children have a place to work on projects or finish homework?

You and Your Caregiver

While all the practical aspects of finding child care are important, the caregiver herself is even more important. Most mothers rely heavily on instinct and intuition in choosing child care.

Although you certainly want to be careful in making a choice, don't be unduly frightened by the publicity given to emotional, physical, and sexual child abuse in day care. The actual amount of such abuse in child care is very low in spite of all the recent media coverage of those cases that have been discovered. Choose carefully, continue to monitor your child's progress and adjustment, and trust your instincts.

How you feel about a prospective caregiver is important. Do you feel comfortable with her or him? Can you talk easily to her about your child and his needs? Does she listen to you? A caregiver who has a lengthy list of rules for raising children probably isn't going to be open to your own views on the topic. Communication is important for both children and adults.

If you are interviewing someone to provide care in your home, does the caregiver seem comfortable in your home? If your housekeeping standards differ greatly, there might be unavoidable conflicts.

The Caregiver and Your Child

Caregivers should be able to listen to what a child says, but more importantly they must be able to sense the unasked questions. A child who says "I won't!" may be feeling "I can't" or "I'm afraid."

Watch how the caregiver reacts to your child. Does she talk down to him? Does she ignore his comments? Or does she really listen to him and encourage him to express himself? Children behave differently when parents are present, so make allowances.

Many caregivers love children—good children, that is! How will the prospective caregiver feel when your child is tired, cranky or behaving badly? Will she be able to love the child while hating the deed?

Does the caregiver reach out to your child? Does she recognize personality and age differences, or does she have strict rules for everyone regardless? A babysitter who loves sweet, docile little girls may not be best with rowdy seven-year old boys. A caregiver who is highly energetic, sportsminded, and extremely vocal may not understand the needs of a timid, quiet child.

Stability is an important factor. Day care providers and babysitters should be willing to provide long-term care, although emergencies can't be predicted. Ask the home care provider how long she has been in business and how long she plans to continue in the job.

Deciding on Discipline

Discipline must be discussed thoroughly with any prospective caregiver. If you are strict and your caregiver is permissive, or vice versa, your child will be confused. Will she be a firm, fair, and loving disciplinarian? Or will she be dangerously doting?

Write down specific questions to ask caregivers about what they expect from children. Do they expect immediate, total obedience? How do they handle behavior problems? What do they do when the children fight with each other? Do they differentiate between outward disobedience and childish mishaps? A child who purposely dumps food because he is angry and a child who accidently spills a glass of milk should be dealt with according to the situation, not the deed.

Discuss the situations that might call for discipline and find out how each would be handled. Do you agree or disagree? If you don't totally agree, is the caregiver flexible in her opinions and willing to work with you so that discipline is consistent with your views? Realize that no two people are going to be in total agreement on discipline. Children do learn that there are different rules for home, school, and sitters, but the differences should not be too great.

Not only should you discuss general discipline, but specific kinds of discipline methods should be agreed on. Regulated home care and centers are not allowed to use corporal punishment. Tell the caregiver what works best with your child. Some children respond to verbal chastening, others need to be separated from playmates until they have calmed down, and older children might be encouraged to make amends for misdeeds. For example, a child who purposely spilled food could be shown how to clean up the mess he caused.

Child Care Centers

Caregivers in centers have the advantage of co-workers to act as buffers throughout the day. If one worker is having difficulty with a child, another can take over. Multiple caregivers also provide more opportunities to match personalities. Children and caregivers often seek out a "kindred soul" and bond together.

When considering a child care center, ask to visit the room where your child will be spending most of the day. Centers often group children according to age so activities and schedules can be planned especially for them. Speak to each of the caregivers and watch them with your child and with the other children.

Are they patient? Do they respond to each child or to only those who demand attention? Do they encourage children to find activities they enjoy or are all children expected to participate in everything?

Ask about staff changes that might affect child care. Because pay for day care workers is low, some turnover is unavoidable, but a high turnover may be indicative of internal problems. Ask about salary schedules and working conditions for aides and teachers. Find out what is being done to improve salaries and benefits in order to keep turnover at a minimum.

Because a center has several caregivers working with a group of children, the departure of a single person isn't as disturbing for a child as a change in both caregiver and physical environment when private care falls through.

Time Will Tell

Pray about your choice before making a final decision. Ask the Holy Spirit to guide you in making the right choice, then continue to pray daily for your family and the people who will be caring for your child.

Once you've chosen a day care situation for your child, give it a chance to work. You all need the time to get to know what works in your new partnership and to work out any small problems. It usually takes about three weeks for everyone to settle in. During this time be sure to ask questions, to make comments, and to make changes.

Talk to your caregiver, your child, and to other parents and children to get a full picture of what is happening when you aren't there. And listen, really listen.

A child who had been in an abusive day care home had told his mother he didn't like it there—many times.

A caregiver who is constantly complaining may be overtired, overly critical, or truly concerned.

Listen with your ears, your heart, and your soul. If you don't like what you hear and your efforts to alleviate the problem fall through, don't be afraid to make a change.

13

Building a Strong Foundation

Child Care Forms and Contracts

Most informal child care arrangements fail because of misunderstandings between caregiver and parent. Even center-based care may be jeopardized when expectations and responsibilities are unclear.

Contracts and policies are the firm foundation of every child care relationship. They are protection for you and your child's caregiver. They formalize your agreement on rates, hours, holidays, vacations, and substitute care. More importantly, they serve as a written reminder of each side's responsibility.

"By the time I chose the center where I finally placed my son, I had looked at so many places that it was difficult to remember who had told me what," said Emily. "The packet of forms and information they gave me was really helpful during those first weeks. If I couldn't remember what the director had said about snacks, I could refer back to their agreement forms. I knew I could always call or ask Timmy's teacher, but it was much easier to have the facts at my fingertips."

Sharon, a licensed day care provider, was glad she had used printed agreements when a client questioned her charge for a holiday. "My contracts clearly state that I get paid for six holidays each year—Memorial Day, Fourth of July, Labor Day, Thanksgiving, Christmas, and New Year's Day," Sharon said.

"When Mrs. Arden received her first bill that included a holiday, she refused to pay for it. When I insisted because that is what we had agreed, her husband got very angry and argued that since I hadn't cared for his son, I shouldn't get paid. But *they* both got paid for the holiday, and it was in the contract that they had read and signed."

The parents finally paid because it was in the contract, but they decided to change caregivers.

"I felt badly about it," Sharon said. "But they agreed to my policy when I accepted their child into care, and I thought it was unfair for them not to honor their end of the contract."

Most parents do read contracts carefully and are diligent about honoring them. Major items such as pay, hours, and holidays will probably be easily remembered, but these items are only a few of the many details on which you need to agree. It is usually the minor details that become major problems when misunderstandings occur.

Centers or family day care providers are required to provide basic information on hours, pay, and policies. All centers and most providers will have printed contracts or agreements plus forms for medical and emergency information and care policies.

Basically there are five forms used in day care:

A. Financial agreement
B. Policy agreement
C. Emergency information and medical permissions
D. Child's personality profile or personal record
E. House rules

If a family member, friend or unregulated babysitter is caring for your child, it is even more important that you have the basics in writing to avoid problems.

The forms printed here are samples of those used in day care centers and family day care homes. Since information and format may vary between providers, you may want to add to or subtract from these to meet your individual needs.

In the Appendix, I have supplied copies of the forms discussed in this chapter. These will aid you in obtaining and providing information that your caregiver may not have considered, especially if she is working independently from her own home.

Financial Agreement

Whenever money is involved, a written agreement is absolutely necessary. Any misunderstanding about fees or payments can destroy an otherwise good working relationship with your caregiver. Consider any agreement you sign as a firm commitment and not one that you can renegotiate when it comes time to pay up.

Every financial agreement should include these basic clauses:

1. Hours child/children will be in care:
____________ a.m. to ____________ p.m.
Days in care: ________________________.

Be specific about the hours and days your child will be in care. If you work 9:00 a.m. to 5:00 p.m. five days a week, you will need a caregiver for those hours plus your commute time. Add ten to fifteen minutes to cover traffic delays. If your working schedule is irregular, you would want to specify that.

2. Fees will be:

_______________ *per hour*
_______________ *per day*
_______________ *per week*
_______________ *bimonthly*
_______________ *monthly*

Hourly and daily fees work best for irregular, part-time, and occasional child care. If you're working on a full-time regular schedule, you will probably opt for weekly, bimonthly, or monthly fees which are generally less expensive.

*3. Overtime will be charged at $*__________ *per fifteen minutes starting at* _______________.

Overtime rates are usually set very high to discourage parents who consistently pick up children late. Generally this rule is enforced only when parents are inconsiderate about observing closing times. I don't know of any center or caregiver who charges late fees for every minor infraction. Remember that centers have to pay overtime to employees who must stay when parents are late. Family day care providers are working mothers who have their own families to care for at the end of their working day.

4. Child's special needs:
additional meals _______________
transportation _______________

Centers and providers generally include lunch and snacks. If your child's needs go beyond this, you will probably be charged extra. Transportation may or may not be included. A center that transports school-aged children to school may include this in their regular rates. Transportation for special outings or those not ordinarily included in regular rates probably will be dealt with separately. For example, if your day care provider takes your child to and from a preschool program or special classes on a regular basis, she may charge for this service.

5. Fees are due ________________________________.
Please pay fees promptly.

Try to have your payments due on or close to your regular pay days. Centers may have all fees due at the same time, but some independent caregivers may be flexible. Budget your child care expenses so they are paid promptly and in full. You don't want to jeopardize a good child care situation because you are forgetful, slow, or unreliable in paying.

*Signed*____
*Date*____

Signatures and dates are important, so don't forget to sign all forms and papers before turning them in! This is your acknowledgement of your child care agreement. If you don't understand something, note it with a question mark and clarify that item before signing.

Policy Agreement

The financial agreement deals with specifics that pertain to individuals. This section deals with general information regarding policies that apply to all parents and children using the day care facilities.

The following points are usually covered in a typical policy agreement made between parents and the caregiver.

a. Except for part-time care, rates include lunch and two snacks. Breakfast and dinner will be provided by special arrangement.

b. Part-time care, less than four hours a day, includes snacks but no meals unless otherwise agreed on. You may bring a sack lunch or pay a small fee if you wish meals included.

c. Full-time care must be paid for on an agreed schedule. Part-time care must be paid for at the end of each session.

d. Full-time clients are charged the regular rate for sick days and the following holidays: New Year's Day, Memorial Day, Fourth of July, Labor Day, Thanksgiving, and Christmas. Two week's vacation per year is allowed without charge. Any time beyond this must be paid for at regular rates to hold your child's place until he returns.

In most child care situations, fees will not be pro-rated if your child leaves before his regular pick-up time.

e. Twelve hour's notice is required for all cancellations for part-time care. If a child or parent is ill, give notification as soon as possible. You will be charged for cancellations without notice and for absence due to illness.

While parents accept these rules when they are dealing with a child care center, some parents object when the same rules are applied by a babysitter or family day care provider. But paying for holidays, paying for non-care to reserve a place for their child, disallowing pro-rated fees, and charging cancellation fees are fair and reasonable conditions for any kind of child care. Be sure to discuss them thoroughly and understand what each side expects from the other person.

Caregivers who work in their own homes should be accorded the same financial courtesies as centers. When they are treated professionally everyone benefits.

One of the common problems individual caregivers run into is the "Grandma's Day."

"Grandma (Aunt Ellen, Cousin Sue) would like to take Billy for the day (the afternoon, a few hours), so I know you'll be happy to have the time off," says the parent.

What she doesn't add is that is she also considers this a savings on her day care bill, and the caregiver will be expected to deduct, or pro-rate, Grandma's Day from her fees.

Like overtime, this isn't a problem if it happens rarely. But most child care providers cannot afford time off without pay. They depend on reliable parents to provide them a consistent income.

f. If we're unable to provide care, we will/will not provide a substitute caregiver or you may choose one. You will not be charged for this time.

g. We will/will not take care of children during the contagious period of an illness. You are responsible for finding someone to care for your child when he is sick. If a child becomes ill while in our care, you will be notified so we may discuss what should be done.

If you are using a child care center, you will probably not have to worry about substitute care, except for illness and holidays that you work when the center is closed. But it is always wise to have someone you can call in an emergency. Independent caregivers may or may not have a substitute ready for an emergency. If your caregiver doesn't, you should ask a friend, neighbor, or family member to stand by.

If your caregiver does provide substitute care, you will want to know who and where. Check out the substitute as you would the primary caregiver.

Sick children need to be at home with a parent if at all possible. But parents can't always stay home unless the situation is serious. Caregivers must be cautious to protect other children in their care. Single parents are especially affected by this dilemma.

Ask what criteria are used to decide when a child will be accepted for care. Fever, vomiting, or diarrhea should be treated at home; sniffles, minor stomach upsets, and non-contagious periods of childhood illness such as measles and chicken pox may be managed by the caregiver under some circumstances.

Be sure you understand when your caregiver will take a sick child and establish alternatives for when you need them.

Some communities have set up innovative "sick-child" programs that range from individual care in the child's home to isolation units staffed by trained nurses at centers. Costs run from expensive to free, depending on the program and a parent's ability to pay.

h. Two week's notice or two week's pay is required to terminate this agreement.

Fair's fair. You wouldn't want to be terminated without notice, and neither does your caregiver. Centers and providers need this notice in order to fill spaces with other children who may be on a waiting list. If you are using an individual caregiver, you might add to your contract that she also give you notice of cancellation.

Initial this bottom portion of our agreement and return the completed form on your child's first day of care. Notify your child's school that I will be caring for him.

If you child attends a school or pre-school, it is important that the proper authorities be informed about who's caring for your child before or after school hours. In case of an emergency, they will know who to contact.

Day Care Register

Emergency information and medical permissions are required by law in all regulated care situations. It must be kept current and available for inspection at all times. The information is for the protection of you and your child and for the convenience of your caregiver.

1. Child's name: ______________________________
birthdate: ______________________________
home address: ______________________________
telephone: ______________________________

2. Parents: ______________________________
home address: ______________________________
telephone: ______________________________
business address: ______________________________
telephone: ______________________________

3. *Person responsible for child if other than parent:*
   home address: ______________________
   telephone: ______________________
   business address: ______________________
   telephone: ______________________

This is standard information. If your child has a step-parent, is living with grandparents or guardian, or if there are older siblings who are responsible for him, let your caregiver know. If you share custody with a former spouse, tell your caregiver how much and when that parent will be involved with your child care arrangements.

4. *Name of person other than parents to call in an emergency if parents or guardian can't be reached:*
   name: ______________________
   home address: ______________________
   telephone: ______________________
   business address: ______________________
   telephone: ______________________

This might be a neighbor or other family members.

5. *Physician:* ______________________
   address: ______________________
   telephone: ______________________

6. *If this physician can't be reached, what action should be taken?* ______________________
____

7. *Emergency hospital address:* ______________________
____

8. *Other:* ______________________
____

9. *Health insurance plan and policy number:* ______
____

The more information you give your provider, the better she will be able to care for your child in an emergency. Some family doctors ask parents to provide emergency care permission statements that are kept in their child's medical records. Talk to your doctor and ask for suggestions on how to best handle emergencies when your child is being cared for by others.

10. *Persons authorized to take child from home:*
Relationship: ______________________
Password: ______________________

Unless another person regularly picks up your child, personally let your caregiver know each time someone else will be taking your child. Talk to her directly and put it in writing, too. If someone calls or shows up with instructions supposedly from you, have your caregiver call you at work. A small bit of bother or embarrassment is not too much to pay for safety.

11. *I give* ______________________ *permission to obtain emergency medical care for my child/children.*

Signed ______________________
Date ______________________

12. *I give* ______________________ *permission to provide transportation for my child/children whenever necessary.*

Signed ______________________
Date ______________________

These are standard permission statements.

Please return this paper completed and signed on your child's first day of care.

Again—don't forget those signatures and get the forms to your caregiver immediately. This information won't do her any good laying on your kitchen counter! Also, if there are any changes in work or home phone numbers or addresses, or changes in family relationships, give your caregiver the updated information.

Your Child's Personal Record

The first days or weeks in child care can be made easier by providing the caregiver with information about your child. Here are some suggestions that will help everyone through the period of adjustment.

Please fill in the following information to help me get acquainted with your child.

1. Does your child have:

Any medical or health problems such as allergies, asthma or diabetes? ______________________________

____

*A fear of animals, the dark, being alone, etc?*____

____

A strong food dislike? __________________________

This information is especially helpful in those first few days of care. If a child is overly quiet or cranky, caregivers can check to see if they are inadvertently causing an upset. Some children are not brave enough to tell the new person in their life that they don't like peanut butter sandwiches no matter how nicely made.

If your child is in a center, they will request information on immunizations. You may have to have a health certificate for your child before he starts care.

2. What are your child's favorite:
foods ____________
toys ____________
games ____________
books or stories ____________
activities ____________

3. Does your child get along well with other children?

4. Does he/she know how to use crayons, scissors, paste?

5. How would you describe your child's personality?
____
____

This information will help your caregiver make those first days enjoyable. Serving a favorite food or reading a familiar story makes a child more comfortable in a new setting. It also helps the caregiver buy useful supplies and equipment. If she is caring for toddlers younger than your child, the notes you filled in about his love of puzzles lets her know she should add some to her collection of toys.

6. Does your child take a nap or need a rest period?
____

7. Please list feeding and nap schedules for infants.
____

8. Is he/she toilet trained? ______________
If not, how do you handle training? ______________
____

Naps and feeding times are important. Ask your caregiver to follow the same schedule you use at home. Toilet training, if it isn't completed before your child enters child care, should be consistent. Ask your caregiver to use the same technique during the day that you use at home.

9. Name and address of child's school: ______________
____

10. School hours: ______________

This important information will help your caregiver plan her day. Neighborhood caregivers will probably know where your child's school is, but a center that doesn't provide transportation may be called to pick up a child at school for some reason (soiled clothing, discipline problems, or illness). They will need to know the school's address. If your child walks from the school to his caregiver, give her an estimate of how long it usually takes so she can judge when a child is overdue and needs to be checked on.

11. What kind of discipline works best with your child:
____

You talked about this in depth when you were hiring your caregiver, now put it in writing so she will have a reminder of how to handle discipline.

Use back of this sheet to include further information.

Depending on the child, you, and your caregiver, you may want to add more. Don't hesitate to go into as much detail as you feel comfortable about. A seasoned caregiver will understand your concerns. If she doesn't, you may need to discuss this and possibly make another choice of caregiver.

If at any time you'd like to discuss your child or his care with me, please set a time when we may talk privately.

Problems should not be discussed in front of children. If your child is in a center, discussions can take place in the office or a conference room. If you have a private caregiver, a phone call in the evening after the children are in bed is a better time for discussions about care, concerns, and suggestions. Compliments are welcome any time!

Please return this completed form on the first day of care.

You may get tired of reading this, but not as tired as caregivers who have to repeatedly ask parents to return forms! Some centers and caregivers will not accept a child until all the forms are signed and delivered.

House Rules

House rules, policies, whatever your caregiver or center calls them, are important for a congenial relationship. Children need to know what is expected of them and so do you.

The following sample of house rules is used in a day care home:

1. Every household has rules. Our family shares our home with you, so please remember that while child care is my job, this is our home. Show us the same courtesy you would expect in your own home.

One of the common complaints from caregivers is the wear and tear on furniture. I've had toddlers write on new slip covers with ball point pens. (I used hair spray to remove it!) I've had six-year-olds stand on sofas and a five-year-old climb onto the kitchen counter to get her mother's attention! Anyone who cares for children expects a certain amount of damage, but children can and should learn to treat furniture, toys, equipment, and even the family pets with courtesy.

Child care centers may be virtually kid-proof, but even there proper behavior is encouraged as part of the maturation process.

2. Sharing is part of growing up, but you can make my job easier if you don't allow the children to bring things from home. If a child brings a toy from home, it will be put aside until he goes home. Special security toys and blankets are welcome at any time.

3. Don't bring food or snacks unless there is enough to share. Check ahead when bringing treats.

Both centers and family day care have regulations about bringing toys and food from home. They may differ in detail, but they are designed to eliminate problems while keeping children happy.

4. It is nearly impossible to please all children at mealtimes. I do expect children to try new foods and to eat reasonably. I do not force children to eat, but I will not allow children to skip nutritious meals and fill up at snack time. If your child is extremely fussy, you may bring a sack lunch for him.

Food should never be used as a punishment and seldom used as a reward. The emphasis should be good nutrition and healthy attitudes.

5. If a child must bring money for school lunches or activities, please put it in a sealed, marked envelope and give it to me. Children love the sound and feel of money, but coins get lost, eaten or stolen. Please do not send money with your children unless absolutely necessary.

Love of money is the root of all evil—especially when it comes to little ones. Please take this rule seriously.

6. Discipline your child while you are in my home. If you don't, I will. No jumping on furniture, running through the house or hitting will be tolerated. If you give your child permission or allow him to leave the house while you are there, you must accept responsibility for him.

Children who behave like angels all day seem to become possessed by demons when parents walk through the door! Part of the reason is they unconsciously sense that the period when parents and caregiver are both present represents a time-warp. They seem to know that the transfer of "power" or discipline is in limbo.

Caregivers hesitate to discipline in front of parents, and parents hate to greet a child they've been away from all day with a host of "no's." But remember that someone needs to be in control for the children's sake.

Caregivers and parents alike have examples of the dangers of "transfer of power time-warp"—children who dash outside when they thought the sitter was watching them, or a toddler locking himself in the bathroom because each adult thought the other was supervising the child.

7. Family day care is special because it tries to duplicate the warmth and love of your own home. Thank you for helping me give your child the best possible care.

"Thank you's" are the magic password that make good child care great. Whether you're using a private caregiver or a center, it is important to show appreciation. Saying "thank you" often and with meaning will also allow a criticism to be accepted more graciously.

Now that you know what to expect from your caregiver and what will be expected from you as a parent, the going should be a little smoother. Placing your child in someone else's care for the majority of the day is a serious step to take. By being informed and knowing what questions to ask, your mind should be more at ease.

14

The First Day

Preparing Yourself and Your Family for a New Adventure

New beginnings are exciting, but they can also be scary. Remember your first day of school? You couldn't sleep the night before; you worried about what to wear; and you wondered whether your old classmates would still be your friends this year.

You may be an adult now, but placing your child in day care brings back all those fears. You've spent hours praying about your decision to go to work. You've researched and evaluated a variety of child care situations before choosing the best possible one. Now it's time to live with those decisions.

On top of all this, you are starting a new job or returning to an old one after being away for awhile. It's only natural to be somewhat nervous and a bit hesitant. What if you misinterpreted God's leading and He really doesn't want you to work now, or at all? Is that day care center really as nice as it looked? Is your sitter (or caregiver) really as capable as you think?

You not only have to deal with your own fears, but you also have a child who may or may not be coping with this change. It's not easy to comfort a tearful child when you're wishing you had a security blanket or pacifier to ease your own doubts.

Where can we turn for comfort and stability in a time of transition? Remind yourself of these words from Psalm 121:

> Where does my help come from? My help comes from the Lord . . . The Lord will keep you from all harm—he will watch over your life; the Lord will watch over your coming and going both now and forevermore—Psalm 121:1-8.

If you look to God for help during this difficult time, He will watch over your children at day care and be with you as you come and go from work.

Are You Ready?

The best way to deal with "first-day" jitters is to be prepared. Day care can be a rewarding experience for parent and child, or it can be a disaster. The difference is often a matter of attitude. A negative, trouble seeking attitude will undermine even the best day care. A positive, problem solving approach can make good child care better and smooth over the glitches in less-than-perfect situations.

First, reassure yourself. You have made the best possible decision based on the information available. You have discussed it with your spouse, and you have both prayed about your decision. You can say to one another with confidence, "If God is for us, who can be against us?" (Romans 8:31).

Second, discard all the old notions about working mothers causing delinquency—they don't. Besides, we all know stay-at-home women who are lazy and uncaring and whose kids are terrors.

The new myths that promote supermomism can be just as harmful. God doesn't expect us to be perfect, so shed those fairy-tale fantasies, too.

Nurture a positive attitude based on reality. Working mothers can be excellent mothers. The real Supermoms are the moms who are doing the best job according to God's standards. Supermoms realize that they can be at peace pursuing God's will instead of being frustrated by striving for perfection. Feel good about what you are doing and project that attitude to those around you.

Third, talk with your family about their expectations of your new lifestyle. Deal honestly with any areas of doubt. Your husband may feel that the decision for you to work is right, yet he may worry about exposing you to the fleshly temptations of the work world. Your child may be both excited and scared about going to day care. Answer questions truthfully, promise to be sensitive to each other's needs, and watch for changes that are disturbing or disruptive.

Loosening the Tie that Binds

Everyone reacts differently to having their child cared for by others. The mothers of Samuel and Moses let others care for their sons permanently. You will only be sharing your child's care for a portion of each day. A first-time mother, insecure about her ability to provide all her child's needs, may be relieved to have an experienced caregiver take over full or part time. A more secure mother may not want to give up control of her child's care, even for a few hours a day. Another mom may want her child to have new experiences found in a day care setting.

"I'd never cared for a newborn before," said Sally, a young first-time mother. "My mother came to stay with me after Brett's birth and when she left, I felt abandoned. I was relieved when my maternity leave was up and I could return to work. Through friends I'd found a warm, loving, older woman to care for Brett. And she adored babies! What I hadn't expected, though, was that Mrs. Johnson also 'cared' for me. She helped me learn about babies, but she never made me feel inept or dumb.

"We plan to have more children," Sally continued, "and I hope to be able to stay home with them eventually. But even if I have to continue working, I know I'll be a better mother because my first day-care experience was a success."

Lydia had the opposite problem. Although she wanted to return to work and had waited until her children were in school all day, Lydia had difficulty turning loose.

"I'd been home with my children for all those early years, and I just didn't believe anyone else could love and care for them the way I did," she admitted. "I know I must have upset my babysitter by always questioning how she handled them. When one of the kids told me they liked her cookies better than mine, I felt rejected."

But because Lydia was basically a secure and caring parent, she was able to work through her feelings and accept that her children could love both her and their after-school babysitter.

"I wouldn't want it any other way," she can say now.

Joan was as excited about her child's entry to day care as she was about returning to her career.

"I stayed home until David was three and ready for pre-school," she explained. "By that time I knew he needed more stimulation than I could give him at home. I was ready for a change, too. He's in a day care center with a pre-school program, and he loves it. My job is easier because I know he's happy, and I'm happy because when we are together we enjoy the time more than when we were both frustrated."

Joan was in touch with her feelings about leaving David in child care *before* she returned to her job. Sally and Lydia weren't even aware of their reactions until they were faced with the realities of being working mothers. Sometimes you can't foresee how you will feel in a given situation, especially not one so emotionally charged as child care. Be prepared to examine those feelings when they come up and prayerfully put them into perspective.

How Long is Long?

Children don't have the experience to evaluate the events in their lives. Their immature and often distorted concepts of time and relationships can create problems.

For example, Timmy didn't mind going to day care—he just didn't expect to have to go every day and all day long. Be specific about the time a child will be at day care. Shelly's mother told Shelly she'd be back for her at five o'clock, but it seemed a long, long, long time before Mommy came to get her.

Find a way to explain "time" to your child. Telling a young child you will be home after her nap and before dinner might be more helpful. In Shelly's case, her mother explained that the first few days might seem long because it was a new experience. She also told Shelly that as she got to know the other children, the time would go by more quickly.

Bryan loved his Mommy, and he loved his babysitter. But he didn't love saying goodbye to one when the other showed up—he wanted them both. Bryan needed reassurance that it was okay to have two "loves" in his life. It was even better than okay. It was terrific that he had two such wonderful people whom he loved and who loved him!

Making the Adjustment

Whether the first-day jitters are your own, your children's, or your husband's, talking about expectations and anxieties before you start work will help ease adjustments.

You can prepare the whole family by reading about other people's experiences. Magazines, even Christian magazines, often have articles about returning to work. Ask your children's librarian if there are any books about working mothers. If not, make up a story about a family whose Mommy works. Use it to illustrate some of the fears your child may be unable to voice. Role playing is also useful.

Try not to make the change too abrupt. When you know you're going to return to work, start leaving your child with a caregiver occasionally so he can get used to your being away. Try to hire your full-time caregiver while you are job hunting so by the time you actually go to work your child will have had time to get adjusted.

Let older family members start sharing some added responsibility beforehand. Encourage children to lay out their own school clothes the night before, and teach them how to make their own lunches. Talk about some of the skills they may need when you are working and practice them. These are all things that children should learn anyway. Children of working mothers just have to learn them a little earlier and a little better.

Even the most modern husband has occasional qualms about working women when it is his wife who is working. Some husbands may want the benefits of an extra income, but none of the inevitable compromises that come with it. A husband may worry about his wife's career becoming more important to her than family or more successful than his own job.

Talk to your husband about your new venture into the working world. Ask him how he feels now that your plans are actually happening. Does he still feel you made the right decision? Is he looking forward to the change, or have some doubts chipped away at his confidence about having a working wife? Discuss how the family will manage the daily responsibilities that you won't be able to do once you return to work. What would be the best way to handle them?

Families with two working parents face problems previous generations never encountered. Balancing everyone's needs isn't easy, but it can work when God is put first. Use God's Word as your guidebook, and keep those prayers moving upward. And again—communicate, communicate, communicate. Don't let problems grow to unsolvable proportions—nip them in the bud with the sharp, incisive shears of God's Word.

Now go forth and work in peace!

15

Partnership Parenting

Making Day Care Work For You and Your Caregiver

One of the most important partnerships you'll ever enter into outside of marriage is the relationship you will have with your child's caregiver. Webster's dictionary defines a partnership as "a legal relation existing between two or more persons contractually associated as joint principals in a business."

Child care is a business. Whether you contract informally with a babysitter to care for your child, or enter a more formal agreement with a licensed family day care provider, a child care center, or some other care service, you are making a business agreement.

Child care, however, is more than just the business arrangement between parent and caregiver. In the legal sense it may be the exchange of services for a fee, but when we are entrusting our most precious children to the care of others—legalities aren't enough. There has to be a sincere caring between parties, the desire to do the best for the child, and a willingness to work together to make child care a loving, positive experience.

A Three-Way Partnership

For day care of any kind to be successful, each person in the relationship has to be considered an equal partner. The child, although not an active party to the actual agreement, is a very important part of the business relationship. Day care in reality is a three-way partnership with each partner having individual expectations.

Parents are looking for quality, loving care for their child. In exchange they expect to pay a fee. The caregiver, whether individual or a group, provides a marketable service for which they expect to be paid. The child expects a safe, happy place to grow.

Each also has a responsibility to contribute something toward making the partnership work. What each will contribute and how they will work together needs to be defined early in the relationship, preferably before the child enters care.

Other business partnerships are required to meet the changing demands of the marketplace. In the same way, your child care partnership must respond to changing needs—the needs of you, your child, and the caregiver. Contracts and agreements need to be re-evaluated on a regular basis to insure that they continue to work for everyone because child care, like parenting, is never really finished.

About the time you think you have everything under control—something (and sometimes everything) changes! And even more important than contracts and agreements, you need to be constantly nurturing the relationship between members of your child care "team."

The apostle Paul told the Corinthians that "the body is not made up of one part but of many" (1 Corinthians 12:14). The key to a successful partnership is remembering that each member is important. Each of you—parent, child, and caregiver—will bring your uniqueness into the relationship. To make all this fit together and work for the common good, it is imperative that you communicate.

Prayer—Your Best Insurance

Pray daily for your caregiver, or caregivers if your child is being cared for in a center. Child care is one of the most emotionally rewarding jobs there is. Nothing is more satisfying than nurturing and caring for a child. Child care is also one of the least financially rewarding jobs. A counter person at a fast food stand often makes more money than a worker in a child care center.

Pray that your child's caregiver is one of those special people who care for children because they love the job—not because it's the only job they can get.

Pray for the center or day care home. Ask God to meet the needs of the caregiver, to watch over the operation of the day care business, and to bless everyone who is involved—the principle caregiver, the aides, the other children, and their parents.

Pray for your child. Pray that he will be protected, loved, and well-supervised.

Pray for yourself. Ask God to direct you in monitoring your child's care for problems that need your attention. Ask for patience, understanding, and wisdom in dealing with any small or large problems that may occur. Don't be ready to deal only with problems, but be quick with praise and encouragement when things go well.

The Personal Approach

Get to know your caregiver personally. Too often caregivers are treated thoughtlessly and quietly ignored as long as they do their job correctly and unobtrusively. This happens to many people in service jobs—waitresses, retail clerks, teachers. Sometimes the only time the people they serve say anything at all is to complain! Make a point to be pleasant, polite, and interested in your child's caregiver at all times.

Ask her what she likes about her job. Find out about her plans, dreams, and interests. Be sincere in your concern, not condescending. You don't need to become best friends, just good allies working for the good of your child.

Having shown personal interest in your child's caregiver makes it less awkward if you do have a question or complaint. It will not only be easier for you to bring up a problem, but it will be easier for her to listen to you.

Talk to Your Child

We are often so busy seeing that our child's needs are met, we forget to ask them what their needs are. Make a point of discussing their needs each day.

In the morning talk about what is going to happen. What is your child looking forward to that day? If he's fearful or concerned about something, find out what and why. What can you do to make it better? What can he do to make it better? Is today "sharing" day? What will he have for lunch?

At the end of the day, talk again. Did the day go well? Whom did he play with? What did he like best today? Your child's answers will help you evaluate, improve, and change his care if necessary.

Even the youngest child can respond to interested questions. All children like knowing that what is going on in their day is important to you. Infants and toddlers may not be able to tell you about their day's activities, but ask anyway to prepare for the day when they can.

Showing You Care

Caregivers need to feel valued. Child care can be physically and emotionally exhausting. If your caregiver is working alone, she probably doesn't get a break, much less a lunch hour. Most babysitters or family day care providers work long hours. Remember their day includes your commute time!

You may not be able to afford to give her a raise or even a bonus, but you can always afford a kind word. Be generous with praise and thank yous. Tell her you appreciate the little things she does for your child—better yet show her!

Many years ago when I was babysitting, I answered my doorbell one evening to find two of my day-care darlings, Danna and Tonya, holding a lovely potted plant. They both yelled (I do mean *yelled*) "Trick or Treat!" and since it was the week before Christmas, we all laughed. The plant died after a reasonable life span, but my fond memories of those little girls and their appreciative parents remained for a long time.

If your child goes to a center, bring the workers a bouquet of spring flowers, send a thank you card, or make a point to tell them how much you appreciate the job they do.

Private caregivers and centers can always use help, financial or otherwise. Ask your caregiver if you could purchase a toy or game to be used by all the children. You might donate your child's outgrown (but not worn out) books, puzzles, or toys to the day care program. Offer to bake cookies for special occasions or pay for ice cream after a field trip.

Non-profit centers often have advisory boards, parenting groups, or fund-raising activities. When you become involved with the operation of your child's day care center, you learn about their needs and problems. You also meet other parents, which also helps you learn more about what is going on.

Are you the only parent who is worried about teacher turn-over? When you talk to other parents, you may discover that your child isn't making up tales about Johnny hitting or Susy stealing.

The best way to change a less-than-perfect day care situation is by working as a group with others. If you don't like the way a center or day care home is operated, you will have more influence in asking for necessary changes if you are part of an organized group.

The Big C—Cooperation

Parents aren't the only ones with complaints. Caregivers frequently complain about parents who don't pay on time, who pick up children late, and who are inconsiderate in many ways. To insure a well-functioning partnership, it is crucial that you consider your caregiver's concerns and be ready to change your own habits if they are causing problems.

"Parents forget that this is my home," said Angela, a family day care provider.

"I want the children to feel comfortable, but I can't allow them to put shoes on the upholstery and run toy cars over the coffee tables. I know their parents don't allow them to behave that way at home. Parents often feel that because I'm being paid to care for children, I should put up with the damage they cause. I try to be reasonable about the amount of wear and tear on our home, but realistically I don't make enough money to replace furniture that could be protected by a few sensible rules."

Angela was frank about how she felt about the children's carelessness, and generally the parents were cooperative. One parent, however, thought she was overly strict.

The parent pointed out that her children were small and that it was difficult for them to sit on furniture without getting their shoes on upholstery. She also said that they *needed* a place to play cars and get a bit messy.

"I know people have different concerns about caring for possessions, and I know children need space to play," Angela told her. "But this is still my home, and after the day care children leave, my family lives here and we entertain our friends here. I take pride in how our home looks. And I also believe that children need to learn to respect their environment at home, in other people's homes, at school, and wherever they are. It's a matter of respect for other people."

Because the matter was openly discussed, both Angela and the parent were able to come to a workable arrangement. The parent donated some large overstuffed pillows for the children to lounge on, and Angela's husband made a play table. Angela set up an area where the children didn't have to be so careful playing.

"I hadn't thought of it from her side," the parent said. "I just thought she was more concerned about keeping her house clean than letting the children enjoy themselves."

"She made some good points," Angela admitted. "I was so close to the situation I hadn't noticed what she saw readily. It took both of us to see the total problem, and it was very satisfying to work the problem out."

Unreasonable Expectations

Caregivers also complain that parents often have unreasonable expectations about their child's care. Some parents are unreliable, and others don't respect caregivers' rights or opinions.

"Sometimes parents expect me to run my home like a nursery school with scheduled activities and crafts everyday," said a babysitter.

One child care director was concerned that some parents expected their children to learn things that should be taught in kindergarten. "The goal of pre-school and pre-school day care is socialization," she said. "We want to get them used to the group situation so when they go to kindergarten they can learn."

"I find that parents pay me last because I'm 'just a babysitter,' said a licensed family day care provider. "They forget that I'm a working mother, too. I depend on my paycheck just like they do."

Centers and home care providers both wish parents were more reliable in paying, picking up children on time, and returning agreement, medical, and change of address forms promptly.

Bias on Both Sides?

One of the most curious problems between parents and caregivers is a subtle, and sometimes not so subtle, discrimination. The discrimination surprisingly goes in both directions—toward the working parent *and* the caregiver!

Working mothers may have gained acceptance today, but it isn't universal.

"Some people still feel that mothers should be at home with their children," said one working mother. "I've had co-workers, supervisors, and even family make pointed remarks about my working. My babysitter feels 'sorry' for me because I have to work. I haven't the courage to tell her I don't have to work for financial reasons, I work because I need to for myself. I don't think she would understand."

On the other side, home caregivers and workers in centers are also put down in a subtle manner. "My working mothers can't understand why I want to stay home," said a day care provider. "I know they think I'm dull and uninteresting." Caregivers are sometimes viewed as "menial" workers whose only role is to wipe noses and clean up spills.

Partnerships can't work without communication, reliability, and respect. Work at including all three in your parenting partnership and remember 1 Corinthians 13:13—"And now these three remain: faith, hope and love. But the greatest of these is love." Love your child's caregiver!

When Your Child's Unhappy

Sometimes the differences aren't between the parent, child and caregiver, but with other children or parents in the group. In centers and group home care where a number of children from different families are mixed, situations can be volatile. Because of the number of people involved, the problems are more difficult to deal with.

Kristi and Michael hated each other. Michael was nine, a bit too old for his home day care, and he hated being put with the younger children. Kristi was seven and a tease. She was also adept at setting Michael up to take the blame for her mischief. Their sitter was aware of their "endearing" qualities and worked hard at keeping them apart.

Their caregiver gave Michael special treatment as the oldest child in the group. She let him pass out snacks, supervise the toddlers, and occasionally paid him a small fee for "helping" to encourage him in mature behavior.

Kristi was encouraged to play with a child nearer her age. When there was no one in the group for her to play with, her sitter let her invite a school friend over.

She also spent a lot of time explaining to both children the rules of social behavior and their rewards, or consequences, if they weren't practiced. If Kristi teased Michael, she should expect him to explode and try to get even. If Michael snarled at Kristi because he was mad at being at a "babysitter's," he knew she would whine and tattle on him for being mean. It was a no-win situation.

The children were unhappy, the parents refused to speak to each other, and the sitter was caught in the middle.

After a few months of trying to work the problem out, it was mutually agreed that Michael should leave. Kristi and her younger sister had been with the sitter longer and had been doing well until his arrival. While it wasn't really Michael's fault any more than it was Kristi's, this seemed to be the only workable solution.

No parent wants their child in a situation where he is unhappy, and no caregiver wants to be a constant mediator between families. When there are conflicts, whether it is between children, parents, caregivers or any combination of the three, sometimes changes have to be made.

When the Partnership Fails

Michael needed a different type of care—one that would better meet his needs. If your child is having problems, and attempts to solve them aren't successful, you need to find a place where he can be happy.

But don't make changes too quickly. Give everyone a chance to make adjustments. Generally, there is a settling in period for any kind of child care. Wait at least three weeks to see how everyone is coping with their new circumstances. Then evaluate the situation, try to formulate a solution, and wait a little longer to see if the solution works.

If you still think a change is necessary, determine if it should be made immediately or whether it can wait. Changes made too quickly without proper preparation and planning can be bad for your child. Unless it is an emergency, take time to study what the problem is and what you need to do to make sure the next caregiving situation will be better.

Try to make the change as easy as possible by leaving on good terms with your caregiver and explaining to your child why you are making the change. If you can, time the change to take place during a holiday or school vacation. Try not to change schools and caregivers at the same time.

If you find that you are making changes in child care often, ask yourself why. You may have to re-evaluate whether you should be working. Don't ever be afraid to make a change when you feel it is necessary. Your child is worth the effort of finding the best possible care.

16

Spotting Trouble

Preventing, Stopping, and Reporting Child Abuse

BABYSITTER CHARGED WITH MURDER

SEXUAL ABUSE DISCOVERED AT CHILD CARE CENTER

CENTER SHUT DOWN—DIRECTOR ARRESTED

We've all seen the headlines. Physical and sexual abuse is reported almost daily in our newspapers, on radio, and on television. Yet child abuse is more likely to occur in the home by a parent, relative, or family friend than in a child care situation by a hired caregiver.

"In 1984, of the one million child abuse cases reported to the American Humane Society, less than one and a half percent were sexual abuse cases involving child care providers or babysitters" (National Commission on Working Women Child Care Fact Sheet).

As concerned parents, however, we must be vigilant in protecting our children no matter where they are. We need to be aware of, and guard against, the abuse of our children. To do so, we must be knowledgeable about what abuse is, how it occurs, and why it happens.

While sexual child abuse, followed by physical abuse, is currently the most highly publicized form of abuse, we must protect our children against abuse of any kind. Emotional abuse, neglect, carelessness, and ignorance may not be physically evident, but they leave invisible scars on children that last a lifetime.

Physical Abuse

Physical abuse may be simple pinching, pushing, or pulling hair or serious physical battering that results in broken bones and internal injuries. Anything that causes physical harm or pain should be considered abusive.

The Bible admonishes us to discipline our sons and daughters. Let's examine a parent's scriptural mandate for raising and disciplining children:

> He who spares the rod hates his son, but he who loves him is careful to discipline him—Proverbs 13:24.

> Do not withhold discipline from a child; if you punish him with the rod, he will not die. Punish him with the rod and save his soul from death—Proverbs 23:13, 14.

> The rod of correction imparts wisdom, but a child left to itself disgraces his mother—Proverbs 29:15.

All these scriptures encourage parents to chasten or discipline an unruly child. Yet there is a difference between discipline and punishment. Discipline teaches and corrects. Punishment only hurts, and too often the hurts cause lifelong damage.

A parent who skips discipline and resorts to punishment only warns the child not to get caught the next time! Nothing is changed or improved.

Discipline is only one side of the coin. Scripture also encourages parents to be loving and nurturing with their children. (See Ephesians 6:4 and Colossians 3:21.) Prudent discipline administered lovingly by a parent does not leave bruises. Most parents will at sometime physically discipline a child with a swat on the backside or judicious spanking. But there is a big difference between a swat or a spanking and physical punishment that is in reality "a beating."

For starters, physical punishment should be administered only by a parent or by a trusted, caring person who has been given that authority by a parent. State and federal child care laws and regulations state that children should never be subjected to physical or unusual punishment, humiliation, mental abuse or punitive interference with daily functions of living such as eating, sleeping, or elimination.

Sexual Abuse

Inappropriate sexual behavior toward a child is one of the most horrible crimes any parent can imagine. Sexual abuse of children may be sexually oriented touching or fondling, exposure of the child's or adult's genitals, and of course, actual or attempted intercourse, oral copulation, or sodomy.

All sexual comments, innuendo, and "jokes" are inappropriate for Christians, whether they are adults or children. "But the things that come out of the mouth come from the heart, and these make a man 'unclean' " (Matthew 15:18).

Sexually explicit books, magazines, music, and television may be acceptable in today's society, but even the most liberal parents want to be the ones to decide what, when, where, and how their child is introduced to such things.

Christian parents certainly don't allow such offensive material in their homes and should be sure their children are not exposed to it elsewhere—especially not in a child care situation. You have every right to ask that these items be kept out of the children's reach. Better yet, I would question whether I would want my children entrusted to a person who had sexually explicit magazines or books in their home or who watched this type of TV or VCR programing.

Emotional Abuse

Emotional abuse can be as damaging as physical abuse. In some cases it may be even more damaging than physical abuse because it is harder to define and detect. A child battered emotionally doesn't have visible scars, but the psychological scarring is just as damaging.

Emotional abuse can be threats, teasing, demoralizing comments, and non-physical punishment out of proportion to the deed. Threatening to spank, to take away privileges, or to stop loving a child is often more damaging than a quick swat—especially if the threats are frequent and/or aimed at terrorizing a child.

For example, a child who is afraid of the dark should never be threatened with being locked in a closet. A child who *isn't* afraid of the dark should not be locked in a closet. No child should *ever* be put in a closet for *any* reason!

Emotional abuse can also be forcing a child to do anything that he fears, from swimming when he's afraid of the water to eating oatmeal when it gags him! Any child who is genuinely afraid or who becomes unduly upset about something should never be forced into a situation that uses that fear against him.

When I was a day care provider, I cared for a little boy who had pronounced food dislikes. Jared wasn't just fussy about food, he would become extremely upset if he had to eat anything he didn't like. For example, he would not eat jam or jelly of any kind. Not only that, but if I used a knife that I had used to make another child's peanut butter and jelly sandwich on Jared's sandwich, he would spot the tiniest speck of jelly and refuse to eat. He also didn't like nuts, raisins, or other "unknown" items in his cookies. He would crumble a cookie to powder to be sure it was "safe" to eat.

Jared's idiosyncrasies began to cause chaos with the other children who couldn't understand why they had to eat carrot sticks and weren't allowed to demolish cookies before eating. It became such a problem to feed Jared a well-balanced meal that his mother and I agreed she would bring him a sack lunch and snacks to avoid the hassles.

If I had ignored Jared's fear and applied the same rules to him—finish the food on your plate, eat your veggies—that I did with the other children, it would have been abusive.

Teasing a child about a physical or emotional problem such as stuttering or bed-wetting is cruel and generally makes the problem worse. Telling a child that he is no good, bad, or ugly are other forms of emotional abuse. Hopefully, few adults purposely abuse children with harsh words. But adults sometimes mistakenly withhold praise to keep a child humble when that very praise enables a child to grow strong.

Non-physical punishment that is out of proportion to the deed can be equally cruel. Donna told me that her brother was once grounded for the entire summer when a napkin he aimed at a wastebasket ended up on the floor instead. The harsh, although well-meaning, discipline in that home affected those children well into adulthood.

"Richard didn't marry until late in life because he'd had such an unhappy childhood," Donna said. "My sister is still going to a counselor, and I worry about being too harsh with my children."

Neglect, Carelessness, and Ignorance

Neglect comes in many forms. Neglect can be ignoring a child's emotional, physical, or spiritual needs. A child who is left to cry learns that his needs will not be met and becomes insensitive to other people's needs. A parent or caregiver who doesn't provide proper clothing and medical care is guilty of neglect.

When children's spiritual needs aren't met, they are left with a void that cannot be filled by all the material blessings in the world. Children need to know about God, His Word, and spiritual lessons.

Children who are neglected emotionally, physically or spiritually learn to meet their own needs in any way they can—sometimes by emotional manipulation, lying, thievery, or physical force.

Children may be victims of carelessness. A child not watched closely around a swimming pool can drown; improper storage of household cleaners may poison; damaged or accessible electric appliances can injure a child. The list goes on and on.

Ignorance, hopefully, is cured with education. The parent who burns a child's hand when he is caught playing with matches should be taught a better way to show the child the dangers of fire. A person who forces a child to eat or withholds food as punishment needs to be shown more effective ways to deal with children.

Preventing Abuse

All the laws in the world cannot prevent child abuse unless there are caring adults to see that they are enforced. Legislators, child care licensing workers, and law enforcement officers can only do their job when we help them. Parents who are in and out of child care centers and day care homes daily must monitor their child's care.

"We can only monitor a home for health and safety," said one county licensing worker. "Parents are in the best position to judge a home because they see it daily. Yet we had one licensed day care home that wouldn't allow parents inside the house once the agreement for care had been made.

"The parents would deliver the children to the door each morning and pick them up at the door at the end of the day. We tried to tell them that parents should be allowed inside so they would know what is going on. The parents told us to mind our own business. It is very discouraging."

Prevention begins first at home, second with choosing our child's caregiver, and third with constant watchfulness. While we will deal mostly with sexual abuse in this chapter, remember that the steps for preventing, identifying, and coping with abuse are the same for all kinds.

What You Can Do at Home

Begin by knowing what child abuse is and why it happens. Children are more often sexually abused by family members or friends than strangers.

Child abusers often show love and caring toward their victims, enticing them with kind words and deeds. Abusers are emotionally ill and reach out to children for the physical and emotional needs they are unable to get from their peers.

The best way to protect your child from any kind of abuse is to build his self-esteem so he can say "no" whenever he feels uncomfortable.

Christian parents teach children to be obedient to parents and respectful to other adults. But like the Christian wife who confuses abuse with wifely submission, our children need to learn to differentiate between obedience to responsible adults and those who might use their "adult" status to harm them.

Linda D. Meyer in her book, *Safety Zone*, says that in teaching our children to always respect, trust, and obey adults, we are putting them in a vulnerable position that is open to assault.

The Safe Child Book, Preventing Child Abuse by Sherryll Kerns Kraiser suggests teaching a child to say no in small things to help them say no when faced with abuse.

"Many children tell me their body belongs to God," the author writes. "I suggest to them that they are partners with God. Children help God to take care of them by taking care of their bodies, brushing their hair, dressing themselves, and keeping themselves safe."

We need to tell our children what is acceptable and what is not and then give them permission to say "no." Both *The Safe Child Book* and *Safety Zone* give good practical help in training parents and children to deal safely with an unsafe world.

For the Christian parent, we need to add the armor of faith and prayer. We also need to caution our children that even Christians can sometimes be abusers and that the same rules of saying "no" apply to Sunday school teachers and other Christian friends.

Check and Double Check

Earlier chapters talked about checklists for choosing child care. You chose the best child care for your child's age and personality. You looked for a caregiver with whom you could work as a partner. You also looked at practical things such as availability, cost, and convenience.

You wanted a safe environment and a caring atmosphere, and you did everything possible to insure that you got both—checked references, made sure licensing or certification requirements were met, and prayed for guidance in making your final decision.

But your job doesn't end with the choosing. It continues as long as your child is being cared for by someone else. Now you need to monitor your child's care every day. Because parents are in and out of the day care situation daily and because they live with the results of a caregiver doing or not doing her job, parents are the best judge of child care.

You Can't Fool All the Parents All the Time

When I was doing licensed family day care, I quickly learned to cope with visiting licensing workers. At that time they never came without calling. Today most visits are still announced, but occasional unannounced visits can be made if a complaint has been issued.

I knew that one supervisor didn't like a too-clean house. She saw it as evidence the caregiver was spending too much time scrubbing and not enough time cuddling kiddies.

Another inspector had a habit of running her fingertips over curtain rods. The caregivers she supervised could never see what dust-free curtain rods had to do with caring for children.

I quickly learned to adjust to their whims. I'm not saying our social workers weren't good at their jobs, only that they were human. Too often their hands were tied when they did find infractions because parents refused to sign complaints; they had too many cases; and some saw day care licensing as a stepping stone to someplace better. At the beginning of the day care crisis in the 1970s, family day care wasn't high on anyone's list of priorities. So—I learned to greet one supervisor with a child in my arms and the inspector with a dust cloth in hand.

But no way could I, or most other providers, fool the parents who saw how we did our job day in and day out. Sue could have told you when I had a fight with my husband, and Georgia knew how my back was doing by the way I held—or didn't hold—her strapping, seven-month-old son.

Parents need to be aware of the nuances in a care situation. Is the caregiver harried and abrupt just today or is it everyday? What is causing it? Is she caring for too many children? If your child isn't getting the individual attention you would like, is it because the center is understaffed or is it poorly managed?

Maybe a caregiver is having family problems or maybe she's not feeling well. Perhaps the center has a large number of employees out with the current flu bug. What, if anything, can you the parent do to make the situation better? More important, how does whatever is happening in the caregiver's life or the center's business affect your child?

Learn to Look and Listen

Is your child happy and content going to his care? Or does he whine and fuss when you get him ready in the morning? Is this a sudden change in his behavior? Or has it been gradual and worsening?

Talk to your child. Talk to your caregiver. Talk to other parents and children who are using the same caregiver.

When the local newspapers reported child abuse in an area day care home, one of the mothers of a child that had been abused appeared on a TV program. To my surprise her son had told her that he'd been "hurt." Since that time I've heard the same statement made in other cases.

Children often "tell" us what is going on, but we don't always listen. Or we listen but don't "hear."

Listen to your child. Talk to him about his day's activities and how he feels about them, about the other children or his caregiver. Listen not only to what the child says, but to the signals behind the words. Does he seem hesitant? Does he tell "stories" about what happened to another child? Maybe he can't say "this happened to me," but he can tell it through the eyes of another child.

Watch his behavior. If your child becomes sexually curious or starts hitting or becoming physically abusive towards toys, pets or others, he may be acting out what is going on in his life. Ask your child where he learned to masturbate. Where did he hear sexual language? Why is he hitting his baby sister or pulling off his teddy bear's arms?

Whether you are mildly concerned about minor changes in your child's behavior or seriously suspicious that something harmful might be going on, get answers.

Talk to your caregiver in a non-threatening way about the problem. Ask if she's noticed changes in behavior. Ask if there have been changes in routine that might be upsetting. Watch how she or he reacts. Are they willing to discuss the matter, or do they discount the situation as unimportant?

The sitter in one abuse case had logical answers to questions and seemed really concerned. She was later convicted of child abuse. It was discovered that she had avoided licensing by constantly moving from area to area. She had a long line of previous charges of abuse and neglect, but because she put on a good front, parents continued to hire her.

Talk to the parents of other children sharing the same child care. Have they noticed changes in their children? Have they observed happenings that coincide with what you've uncovered? There is strength in numbers. What one parent may dismiss as an isolated incident takes on importance when another parent has had a similar experience.

No one wants to encourage a witch hunt. Don't spread rumors or innuendo based on "suspicions" alone. But don't neglect to follow your instincts, either. If your suspicions can't be confirmed and you still feel uneasy, make a change anyway. Tell other parents why you are leaving so they will be watchful. Make it clear you may be wrong, and you hope you are, but under the circumstances you are more comfortable finding other care.

Signs of Abuse

The Crime Prevention Center of the Office of Attorney General lists the following signs of abuse:

1. Stained or bloody clothing.

2. Major changes in school performance and sleeping patterns, including the onset of nightmares or a sudden fear of falling asleep.

3. Compulsive masturbation or unusually seductive behavior with classmates, teachers, and other adults.

4. Age inappropriate behavior such as bed wetting or thumb sucking.

5. Sudden acquisition of money, clothes, or gifts with no reasonable explanation. Some pedophiles will shower their young victims with presents as one way of enticement.

6. Physical injury or irritations to the genital area, such as pain, itching, swelling, bruising, bleeding, cuts, or scrapes.

7. Halting attempts to tell a friend or trusted adult such things as "I know someone" or "What would you do if . . ."

Reporting Abuse

All forms of abuse can continue only when we choose to let them continue. Yet reporting abuse is difficult. Within families and among friends, abuse may be so complex and entangled in family relationships that there may be the inclination to say or do nothing.

Reaching out for help in making this decision may create more problems. All professionals who work with children are required to report suspected abuse. If you decide to go to a teacher, doctor, or day care director, they are required by the Mandatory Reporting Law in all fifty states to report that abuse is suspected.

Your first concern will be for your child. It is natural to want to protect him or her from further assault by legal procedures necessary to report an offender. Yet people who abuse children sexually, emotionally, or physically do not stop unless someone does something to stop them. You may be able to protect your own child from further abuse by changing day care, but what about the next child who comes in contact with the abuser?

Protecting Your Child When Reporting Abuse

First, let your child know that you believe them and that you will help them. Because abuse is such a traumatic experience, children need all your support plus reassurance that you will make the abuse stop.

Second, contact a person who specializes in dealing with abuse, preferably someone who works with children. If the child is old enough, let him participate in making the decision whether to report it. Always be honest with him about what is happening and will happen.

Third, get professional counseling for your child and your family. Abuse affects the entire family. Every member will need help in dealing with what has happened and what will happen once you report it. A good Christian counselor will help your entire family.

The Safe Child Book has an excellent section on reporting child abuse. It points out that neither child nor parent is responsible for what happens in sexual abuse. The abuser must accept the total responsibility.

No child should be in a situation that isn't loving and supportive. Let caregivers know that your child is to be treated with respect. Don't allow him to be teased or bullied by caregivers or other children in the home. Insist that he be treated fairly, supervised properly, and disciplined wisely. If caregivers are unwilling or unable to give the quality child care you want, find someone who can and will.

Be honest and fair in your evaluation of care, but do report anything serious to the proper authorities.

As Christian parents we want the best for our children. No one can give us a guarantee, but we can use the knowledge that is available and the armor of faith and prayer to cover our children against what we can't control.

17

When All Else Fails

Creative Child Care Alternatives

Sometimes no matter how you plan—nothing works. Babysitters quit. Day care centers don't have openings. You can't afford to stop working. You still need child care—sometimes desperately—and there just doesn't seem to be any available.

To paraphrase an old saying—when the going gets tough, the tough get creative! Women are known for making things work when the odds are against them. So put on your thinking cap and use the following information to create your own day care.

Shared Care

Family day care providers often quit because they can't get enough regular day care clients to provide *them* with a reliable income. Talk to other working mothers who might be having the same problem and hire a provider to care for all your children in her home or yours.

First, look at your current child care situation. What do you like about it? What don't you like? How does it fit your child care needs? If you've had several care situations, pick out the best points of each one and try to find a new situation that will include all of these positive factors.

You may have liked the convenience of the at-home sitter, but felt your child needed the stimulation of other children. The family day care home you used might have provided playmates for your child but not the stability you needed on a regular basis. Or the center may have been reliable and fun for your child, but its location was too far away from work or home.

Second, find one or more women who might be interested in sharing a sitter. Perhaps a co-worker or neighbor also has had trouble keeping quality day care. Perhaps you've met parents at the day care center who liked the center's concept, but not how it was implemented.

Third, meet with prospective care-sharers to study your individual needs and to discuss how you can work out a plan that will work for your group. Perhaps one parent has an infant who needs individual care; another parent may have a toddler who requires close supervision along with freedom to explore and grow. Your older child may need lots of activities to be kept happily occupied. What kind of care would work best for you as a group?

Do you agree on the type of care you want? Do you want an emphasis on spiritual training? Does one parent want a "milk, cookies, and a hug" caregiver while another wants a caregiver who will provide pre-school type activities and a more structured environment? Do you think you will be able to find what you each want in one day care environment? Maybe, but probably not.

Fourth, have a clear idea of what you want and how you plan to achieve it. Then put it all into writing so there will be no misunderstandings about your goals. Written guidelines are also essential to clarify how you will handle hiring, monitoring, and paying for group child care.

Fifth, advertise, interview, and select a caregiver. Check references carefully. Be sure you understand the legalities of hiring someone to come into your home. If you hire a caregiver to come to a private home, you will have to know about paying into social security, state disability insurance, and unemployment insurance. Check out liability insurance. Will your homeowner's insurance cover your caregiver while she works in your home? If not, what kind of insurance do you need to protect your home and family?

As a group you will want to decide on what benefits you might offer the caregiver, such as paid vacations, holidays, and sick pay. The better package you can put together, the better chance you'll have of getting a stable, reliable caregiver who will save you from the constant turnover you may have experienced in other care.

This is a very simplified format for shared care, but like any other business arrangement it is anything but simple. Be thorough in your planning and careful in its implementation. A free child care resource, referral, and support service in Oakland, California has an excellent sixteen-page handout about shared care. If you can't find a resource for information in your own area, order *Parent-Created Child Care—Shares* from Bananas, Inc., 6501 Telegraph Ave., Oakland, CA 94609. Please enclose one dollar to cover printing and mailing costs.

What About Older Children?

Children between the ages of nine and twelve fall between the cracks of conventional day care. A family day care center filled with toddlers and preschoolers can be boring for the older child. After-school care programs that are ideal for the older child sometimes close down during holidays and summer vacations when they are most needed.

If you're using family day care, try to find a home with older children—perhaps a schoolmate's mother who does day care or one with teenage children in the family who can act as big brothers or big sisters.

Hire an older teenager or college student to provide care but don't call it "babysitting!" Presenting care for the older child as "companionship" makes it more palatable. If you're hiring a teenager, be sure that he or she is older than your child and mature enough to exercise proper control. This type of care should be fun, but you don't want to end up having *two* kids getting into mischief!

Your church young people's group may have someone who is good with children and who is willing to make the relationship interesting. Plan activities for them to do together so both will have a good time. Bowling, swimming lessons, and helping with vacation Bible school can be fun when you're a partner with a respected young person.

Knowing When to Let Go

Most parents would prefer never to leave a child on his own. There does come a time, though, when we have no other choice or when the child really is ready to be given responsibility for his own care.

The most difficult part of self-care is determining when a child is ready to be on his own. Individual children mature at different rates. Some children are ready to be on their own at ten; others may need supervision long past that.

Self-care for siblings is even more complicated. One child may be ready while another is not. Some older children are good caregivers for younger siblings. Other children may resent being responsible for a "baby" sister or brother.

How the children get along with each other will also affect your decision on whether to let them care for themselves. Children who fight constantly should have a strong caregiver who can mediate. You may find that having a caregiver for a younger child and letting an older child stay alone may work for your family.

A general guideline is to look at the child's current and past behavior. Has he proven to be responsible? Does he show good judgment in unusual situations? Does your son or daughter panic if things go wrong? You also want to look at your neighborhood—is it a safe place to be on your own? Are there other adults nearby to help in an emergency?

If you decide your child is ready to be on his own, proceed cautiously. Try it for short periods of time first. An occasional afternoon alone after school, an early evening while you go out to dinner, and one or two days with close supervision from you via phone will let you see if your child can handle being on his own.

Always provide detailed, clear instructions about what you expect from them, how they can reach you, and what to do in an emergency.

Busy children have less time for mischief. Plan some after-school chores that have to be done, a time for homework, and an occasional break from routine. During the summer sign the children up for swimming lessons, recreation department activities, and camp. Schedule visits with grandparents to break up the long blocks of time.

As with any kind of day care, be prepared to make a change if you see it isn't working.

Working Solutions to Day Care

Sometimes changing how and where you work can solve your day care problems.

Flextime or rearranging traditional business hours can be one solution. Work shorter hours. If your children are in school, ask your employer if you can work the hours they're at school. You may have to sacrifice some employee benefits, but if your husband has health insurance and a retirement fund, this is a minor, and probably temporary, adjustment to insure your children are well-cared for.

Work different hours. Some employers will allow you to come in earlier or work later as long as you put in a full day. If both husband and wife can adjust their schedules, one can go in early to be off in time for after-school care, the other can go in late to see them off in the morning.

Work at home. With today's computer technology, a terminal and a phone can enable many workers to function at home as well as in an office. You may be able to work half a day at home and half a day at the office.

Job sharing is a new and increasingly popular concept. It is particularly popular with teachers. Those who have pioneered job sharing found they were more successful in getting school districts and employers to accept the concept when they presented a well-planned proposal. Talk to those who have been successful and those who found it didn't work. Find a partner, although this isn't always necessary, and work out a plan. Include how you will share the pay, benefits, holidays, and how you will handle emergencies before presenting it to your employer.

Be prepared to sell the idea with good solid information. If it isn't accepted the first time, try again later. *New Ways To Work,* 149 Ninth Street, San Francisco, CA 94103 has a number of publications on different aspects of job sharing. Write for their brochure.

Mixing Babies and Business

Do diapers and data bases mix? You won't know until you try, and it may be worth a little experimenting to see if it does. Children at the workplace probably do best in small businesses where informality and flexibility are the norm—or if you're the boss!

In our area I know:

1. A grandmother taking care of her grandchild while running a ceramic shop out of her home.
2. A young mother who brings her infant to the small gift shop where she works.
3. A local family counselor who created a nursery in her office for her child and then hired her mother to care for the baby while she was with clients.

The possibilities are endless!

Employer Sponsored Day Care

When most people think of employer sponsored day care, they picture an on-site center. This is only a very small part of the employer sponsored day care available. Most businesses do not have the facilities or finances to have their own day care program.

Hospitals, very large corporations, and business complexes are generally the forerunners in on-site care. They've found it cuts absenteeism and employer turnover to have child care available for employees.

Those employers who don't provide on-site care may offer other services for working parents, such as vouchers or credits to off-site day care facilities that have contracted to provide child care for employees; a child care allowance chosen from a "menu" of employee benefits and/or child care referrals.

A "menu" of flexible options allows workers to choose from a list that can include child care benefits as well as medical coverage and other options. Some benefits may be standard, with others optional. For two-paycheck families that otherwise would have duplicate medical coverage, choosing a day care benefit in place of another health plan may be more sensible.

Resource and referral services provide employees with help in finding day care. A company may hire an outside agency to advise employees on day care or they may hire a day care counselor to help employees find and keep child care. Day care counseling usually includes information on what kind of low cost or free child care is available.

Grants to workers in the form of vendor programs or vouchers toward full or partial cost of day care is another way employers can help with child care. A voucher system gives employees an amount to be spent on child care of their own choice. In a vendor program employers buy child care slots in existing off-site facilities for use by employees.

If your company doesn't already have child care or some of these other services available, you may want to present a plan to the company—or your union. Gather information about successful programs elsewhere, come supplied with facts and figures that demonstrate the benefits to the company, and be prepared to answer questions in a positive rather than negative manner.

If, after a reasonable discussion, your company can't or won't help with child care in some way, you may wish to change employers to one who already offers the services you need or who is willing to start a program.

Community Action

Because the current shortage of child care has become a national issue, you may want to become a community activist and work toward solving the problem for others as well as for yourself.

Association of American University Women and League of Women Voters both have done local, state, and national studies on child care. Our local chapter of AAUW funded a Parent Information Network that provided resource and referral service for all kinds of child-related issues from medical care to play groups. Members of both organizations have served on study groups in the community to look at and resolve child care shortages.

Communities faced with not enough child care have appointed task forces to study what can be done. One of the ways being studied is a development tax to mitigate the need for child care created by increasing commercial development. Housing developers already pay such mitigating fees for roads, trees, and schools. The child care tax would work similarly. You may want to serve on such a study group or work with city government.

As an individual you can talk to your church about starting a child care center or join with your school's PTA to look into latchkey programs.

You may even want to become part of the solution rather than the problem by becoming a day care provider yourself. More about that next!

18

Child Care as a Career

How to Know if it's Right for You

If you're a working mother who's tired of fighting the child care hassles, you may want to consider a career change that will help alleviate the problem for yourself and for other moms who work.

"I'd rather be a babysitter than hire one," said one young mother who had enough of battling babysitters. "One sitter ignored all my instructions. If the children didn't want to take a nap, she didn't make them take one. She didn't care that they were overtired and cranky when I came home. If I said no snacks, she gave them anyway. Another sitter was insensitive to the children's feelings. She made fun of them when they were afraid or shy. I didn't want the children to be in a day care center, either. I finally decided to stay home with my children and become a babysitter for someone else."

Babies are Big Business

With more and more women working outside the home today, service jobs are an expanding field. Restaurants, fast food establishments, and take-out services provide meals for families too busy or too tired to cook after a long day at work. Window washers, housekeepers, and gardeners formerly were hired only by the very wealthy. Today they are common household helpers in two-paycheck homes. In our expanding service economy day care is one of the most rapidly growing services. Without day care there couldn't be as many two-paycheck families.

Any kind of child care, much less the quality care parents want for their children, is in short supply. Communities are asking business developers to include child care facilities in office and commercial complexes. City governments are studying innovative ideas for creating and paying for child care.

The one largest source of day care that you don't hear too much about, although that is rapidly changing, are the mothers themselves! Granted, one woman taking care of two or three children isn't going to make much of a dent in the enormous day care shortage. But if enough women chose to do home child care, it would help.

Is Day Care for You?

Many working mothers find that the emotional or financial satisfaction of a career outweighs any day care problems. If you truly love your job, you will be happier finding ways to continue working. If you have a career where staying out of your field for an extended period of time puts you at a disadvantage, you will probably want to work through child care problems and remain on the job. If you are a happier and healthier person when you work, you won't be content at home.

Some women, though, do not enjoy working. They don't have *careers*; they have *jobs*. Careers are exciting; jobs are what you do to get a paycheck because you need the money. There are a lot of women with jobs who would much rather be home with their children.

If you love being home and you truly enjoy being a full-time wife, mother, and homemaker, babysitting or family day care may become a new and exciting career for you!

By trading a job you don't really like for a new "career" as a family day care provider, you can eliminate your own child care problems, provide yourself with a reasonable income, and help another mother who works out of enjoyment or necessity.

Consider becoming a day care provider if:

1. You would rather be home than working at an outside job.
2. You enjoy children—your own and those of other people.
3. You could use extra income, but you don't need a large amount on a steady basis.

Can You Be a Better Babysitter?

Child care isn't a job for just anyone, though. Some people don't want the responsibility of caring for other people's children, and some shouldn't be caregivers.

Day care is serious business whether you are a parent or a parent substitute. Children aren't products on an assembly line that can be tossed on the scrap heap when mistakes are made and another stamped out with mechanical precision. Bad or inadequate child care is a crime against God and society. While we may not always have a choice about parenthood, we do have a choice when it comes to caring for other people's children.

Child care—good child care—isn't easy, but it is satisfying if you have a real love for children and enjoy being around them. Before you take the plunge into every-day care, however, there are some questions you need to ask yourself.

Do you really like children, or only the "good" ones? Children are enchanting. They can be cute, funny, lovable, and sweet. They can also be horrible little monsters. They spill things, mess up your life, and create absolute havoc. Even the most loving parent can become disillusioned. If you have trouble loving your own child when he's acting "unlovable," it's even harder when someone else's child is being bad and you can't send him home!

Are you in tune to children's feelings? People usually consider a child good if he doesn't create waves. But is a child who doesn't cause any disturbance really good, or is he scared, insecure, or overly passive?

Are you able to accept all children? If a child doesn't conform to your own ideals, can you love him in spite of his idiosyncrasies or handicaps? Can you deal with the trials and tests that mark every child's growth to adulthood?

Are you willing to learn more about children? To be the best caregiver, you will need to read, study, and perhaps even take a class or two in child psychology or child development. You would expect excellence and professionalism from your own child's caregiver, so you should be willing to train yourself in all areas of child care. When you learn about the different age and personality-related behaviors, you will be better equipped to handle them when they occur. You may have experienced these behaviors with your own children, but not all children are alike—even your own are not identical. Each child is different and requires special treatment.

It's the Family's Business

Talk to your family to see how they feel about your becoming a caregiver. Discuss what this would mean to the family. You'll be home to meet their needs, but you won't be able to maintain the same level of attention and efficiency you would if you were just caring for your own family. You will still need their cooperation just as you did when you were working outside the home.

How does your husband feel about having other children around when he comes home at night or sits eating his breakfast in the morning? Working mothers may work nine to five, but you'll be working from eight to six—or longer!

Will your children mind sharing you, their home, and their toys? There are ways to make all this sharing easier, but they need to know what is expected of them before you start.

Coping with Conflicts, Clutter, and Chaos

Working at home does solve your day care problems, but it certainly doesn't solve all the other problems working mothers face.

Babysitters and family day care providers are working mothers with the same conflicts between job and family. While the mother working outside the home feels guilty for being away from her family, the work-at-home mother feels guilty about neglecting her family while working at home! All working women have difficulty doing the best they can at work and at motherhood. It doesn't make much difference where they work.

Working at home allows you to keep your own household functioning fairly smoothly. Take note of the qualifying "fairly" in the previous sentence! Don't expect the same level of tidiness you'd have with just your own family. All those extra kiddies bring the additional clutter of toys, fingerprints on the woodwork, spilled milk, and crumbled cookies.

You can cope with all the clutter by learning to organize just like you did when you worked outside the home. You get up a bit earlier to make the beds and swab the toilets before the children arrive; you delegate tasks to family members; and you cut back on anything that isn't absolutely necessary.

While a good part of your day will consist of only child care, which is what you're getting paid for, you will still be able to do some of your ordinary housecleaning at the same time. You can mop and dust while the children are napping; you can keep the washing machine working on the family laundry while you supervise the children at play; you can bake a batch of cookies with the children and call it a learning activity! You learn how to combine the best of both worlds.

You will need patience with a capital "P." Households with children do not run smoothly. Homes with day care children in addition to their own are chaotic. Efficient planning helps, but be prepared for the best planned day to go wrong.

Parents arrive too early or too late; children forget lunches, coats, and school work. Measles, mumps, and chicken pox crop up unexpectedly. You run out of milk, bologna or—heaven forbid—peanut butter; and by the time you get the breakfast mess cleared away and beds made, it's time for lunch.

All parents need patience, compassion, and flexibility, but day care providers need them in extra-large, industrial-strength quantities.

Can You Afford It?

You can make a good income at child care. Sometimes.

Be realistic about how much income you need to be able to quit working full time to become someone else's child care provider. If you've been working at a low-paying or middle-income level, you can probably make enough money doing child care to balance your family budget.

A woman employed outside the home spends up to half of her income on transportation, lunch, wardrobe, and child care fees. Doing home child care will eliminate those expenses, but you will have to spend more on food, utilities for cooking, laundry, and all that water for washing faces, towels, and flushing toilets!

Because the women who become day care providers are usually home and family oriented, you may be able to save on the family food budget by spending more time to plan and cook meals. Those nice pots of soup, homemade casseroles, and long-cooking pot roasts are easier to do when you are working at home. You may also have more time for sewing family clothing and making gifts and doing your own household repairs.

When I was working outside the home, I spent six hundred dollars on a new sofa and a hundred and fifty dollars on an antique hall tree. When I was doing home child care, I reupholstered an old sofa for one hundred dollars and bought thrift shop furniture to refinish. My finished projects were equally attractive at a fraction of the cost of my store-bought purchases. Cutting down on entertainment and dining out will also help you stretch your at-home earnings.

Do be realistic about your needs and your wants. If you want new rather than recycled furniture, if you like to go out to dinner frequently or take the family on skiing trips, you may not be able to afford such luxuries on an income from home child care.

Don't think you can eliminate "working-mother guilt" by working at home. You still may not be able to serve as third grade's homeroom mother, but you probably *will* find time to bake cookies for school parties. Your home may be messier than when you were working and no one was there during the day, but at least your own children won't come home to a dark house. You will probably still be too tired at the end of the day to give your husband all the tender loving care he needs, but you may manage to have dinner ready on time.

Work-at-home mothers, like those who work outside the home, need to weigh the benefits against the problems and decide what will work for you and your family.

If you're willing to work at establishing yourself, and if you can afford to wait until the word gets around that you are terrific with kids, you could make more than at your previous job. Child care is like any other business—it takes time to get started, and there are risks. Some providers start out earning a good income and continue without any problems. Others take a long time getting established, and others never make it work.

Getting Started

Find out if there is a need for child care in your community. Licensing agencies should be able to tell you the current status of child care availability. Generally, infant and after-school care is in big demand. Some neighborhoods are saturated with sitters, licensed or otherwise, and some desperately need more.

Child care regulations vary across the nation because each state decides whether and how to regulate family day care. Counties and cities add their own rules and regulations. If you want to work at home, you need to find out what your area requires and comply to their standards. Our state requires licensing only if you are taking care of children from more than one family. Some states require certification rather than licensing. Other states don't have any regulations at all.

Learn the going rates for different kinds of child care—infant, preschool, after school, single child, and more than one child per family.

Consider how many children you would need to care for to meet your financial needs. It's better to start out slow—in fact, you may have no choice at first—and see how it works for you and your family.

Talk to someone about contracts—the ones in this book were provided by local caregivers—and then look for clients who need your services.

The same techniques you used in finding a caregiver for your child will work in this case but in reverse. Advertise in the newspaper and tell friends and neighbors you are available. You will also want to contact schools, doctor's offices, and local businesses.

What kind of child care do you want to provide—simple, loving care or a preschool atmosphere? Determine how many children you'd like to care for and what ages are best suited for you and your family. Generally, everyone is happier if you care for children the same age or younger than your own.

Have Reasonable Expectations

Laurel is a classic example of a beginner in the child care business. She calculated the dollars and cents of caring for children in her home, but the reality doesn't always add up as neatly as the figures in a tidily balanced checkbook.

Laurel lived in California's famous Silicon Valley (an area saturated with computer manufacturers and companies) where child care of any kind was at a premium.

After applying for and receiving her day care license, she had contracts printed, passed out fliers announcing her entry into the day care world, and waited for the phone to start ringing.

She planned to hold a meeting for the prospective clients to explain fees, the hours she would operate, and what kind of child care she would provide. Laurel wanted to offer more than just babysitting, so she planned a mini-preschool with story times and play activities. At the end of the meeting she would accept applications from the parents who wanted her services and then *she* would choose the ones *she* wanted to work with.

Her plans, however, did not go that smoothly. Laurel did get numerous calls in response to her fliers, but they were spread over a period of weeks and months. Many people couldn't afford her high rates, even if it was for "quality" care. The callers often specified hours that Laurel didn't want to work—arrivals as early as five-thirty in the morning and departures as late as seven o'clock in the evening. Some even needed evening and weekend care.

Laurel had planned to care for her maximum of six children, each from six different families at seventy dollars per week. The parents who called, however, had two and three children and wanted substantially reduced rates for the additional siblings.

When Laurel finally signed up six children, they were all infants or toddlers. There were two sets of siblings and two other children from separate families. Although she did have to reduce her rates slightly, Laurel made a nice earning from her child care business.

But she didn't last long because she overloaded herself with children in order to match her previous earnings at a computer company. When she became pregnant with her second child, Laurel went back to her old job and paid her mother to watch her sons plus two of the children she'd been caring for.

An established caregiver can make good money, but it takes time to get established. Flexibility is a must, especially in the early stages of business. Then just about the time you think you have the perfect mix of children—parents and children get along with each other and your own family, the hours are great, and the income reasonable—one family may move, another may decide the children can now care for themselves, and your income plummets.

Home day care at its best can be unstable. It's not for the family who needs a specified amount every month. It is great for the family who needs extra income but who can tighten the budget-belt when things fall apart temporarily.

The Choice is Yours

If you believe that becoming a babysitter will work for you, give it a try.

Be willing to work hard and to make changes when necessary. Like working outside the home, change is the name of the game. You may like child care but not a particular child or parent. You may decide you want younger, older, more, or fewer children. You may want to change how you manage your child care business.

Like working, you need to constantly evaluate how you are doing and how what you are doing affects your family and home life. When something doesn't work, examine it, look for a solution, try the solution, and re-evaluate. Don't give up too soon, but don't continue if it really isn't working and changes won't make it better.

The choices are yours, but you have the love and

wisdom of our Lord to help you make the best possible decision for every one.

> Trust in the Lord with all your heart and lean not unto your own understanding: in all your ways acknowledge him, and he will make your paths straight—Proverbs 3:5, 6.

Throughout my life as a Christian, this one verse has been a guide and comfort to me. It isn't easy being a parent, and the choices we make aren't always as clear as we'd like them to be. But because I trust the Lord, I am assured that all my choices are the right ones for me.

Each choice has taught and perfected me, and each choice has renewed and strengthened my faith. I no longer worry about making right choices, I just make the best decision I can and leave the rest to my Lord.

No matter what your choices, I pray that you, your children, and the people who care for them will look to the Lord and learn to trust Him. He can make your paths straight—even *when* Mother must work.

Appendix

Child Care Forms and Contracts

Financial Agreement

1. Hours child/children will be in care:
   ____________ a.m. to ____________ p.m.
   Days in care: ________________________________

2. Fees will be: ________________________ per hour
   ________________________ per day
   ________________________ per week
   ________________________ bimonthly
   ________________________ monthly

3. Overtime will be charged at $________ per fifteen

minutes starting at ______________________________.

4. Child's special needs:
   additional meals ______________________________
   transportation ______________________________

5. Fees are due ______________________________.
Because financial agreements are tailored to individual needs, please pay fees promptly.

Signed ______________________________
Date ______________________________

Policy Agreement

a. Except for part-time care, rates include lunch and two snacks. Breakfast and dinner will be provided by special arrangement.

b. Part-time care, less than four hours a day, includes snacks but no meals unless otherwise agreed on. You may bring a sack lunch or pay a small fee if you wish meals included.

c. Full-time care must be paid for on an agreed schedule. Part-time care must be paid for at the end of each session.

d. Full-time clients are charged the regular rate for sick days and the following holidays: New Year's Day, Memorial Day, Fourth of July, Labor Day, Thanksgiving, and Christmas. Two week's vacation per year is allowed without charge. Any time beyond this must be paid for at regular rates to hold your child's place until he returns. Fees will not be pro-rated if your child leaves before his regular pick-up time.

e. Twelve hour's notice is required for all cancellations for part-time care. If a child or parent is ill, notify me as soon as possible. You will be charged for cancellations without notice and for absence due to illness.

f. If I'm unable to provide care, I will/will not provide a substitute caregiver or you may choose one. You will not be charged for this time.

g. I will/will not take care of children during the contagious period of an illness. You are responsible for finding someone to care for your child when he is sick. If a child becomes ill while in my care, you will be notified so we may discuss what should be done.

h. Two week's notice or two week's pay is required to terminate this agreement. I will give two week's notice if I decide I can no longer care for your child. If I cannot give you notice, I will arrange for two week's substitute care.

Initial this bottom portion of our agreement and return this completed form on your child's first day of care. Notify your child's school that I will be caring for him.

Day Care Register

1. Child's name: ______________________________
   birthdate: ______________________________
   home address: ______________________________
   telephone: ______________________________

2. Parents: ______________________________
   home address: ______________________________
   telephone: ______________________________
   business address: ______________________________
   telephone: ______________________________

3. Person responsible for child if other than parent:
   home address: ______________________________
   telephone: ______________________________
   business address: ______________________________
   telephone: ______________________________

4. Name of person other than parents to call in an emergency if parents or guardian can't be reached:
   home address: ______________________________
   telephone: ______________________________
   business address: ______________________________
   telephone: ______________________________

5. Physician: ______________________________
   address: ______________________________
   telephone: ______________________________

6. If this physician can't be reached, what action should be taken? ______________________________

____

7. Emergency hospital address: ______________________
____

8. Other: ____
____

9. Health insurance plan and policy number: ______
____

10. Persons authorized to take child from home:
Relationship: ________________________________
Password: ___________________________________

11. I give ______________________________ permission to obtain emergency medical care for my child/children.

signed ______________________________________
date ____

12. I give ______________________________ permission to provide transportation for my child/children whenever necessary.

signed ______________________________________
date ____

Please return this paper completed and signed on your child's first day of care.

Your Child's Personal Record

Please fill in the following information to help me get acquainted with your child.

1. Does your child have:

   Any medical or health problems such as allergies, asthma or diabetes? ______________________

   ____

   A fear of animals, the dark, being alone, etc?

   ____

   A strong food dislike? ______________________

2. What are your child's favorite:

   foods ______________________
   toys ______________________
   games ______________________
   books or stories ______________________
   activities ______________________

3. Does your child get along well with other children?

   ____

4. Does he/she know how to use crayons, scissors, paste?

   ____

5. How would you describe your child's personality?

   ____

   ____

6. Does your child take a nap or need a rest period?

   ____

7. Please list feeding and nap schedules for infants.

   ____

8. Is he/she toilet trained? ______________________
If not, how do you handle training? ________________
____

9. Name and address of child's school: ____________
____

10. School hours: ______________________________

11. What kind of discipline works best with your child?
____
____

Use back of this sheet for further information.

If at any time you'd like to discuss your child and his care with me, please set up an appointment when we may talk privately.

Please return this completed form on the first day of care.

House Rules

1. Every household has rules. Our family shares our home with you, so please remember that while child care is my job, this is our home. Show us the same courtesy you would expect in your own home.

2. Sharing is part of growing up, but you can make my job easier if you don't allow the children to bring things from home. I have a varied supply of toys and playthings. If a child brings an item from home, it will be put aside until he goes home. Special security toys and blankets are welcome at any time.

3. Don't bring food or snacks unless there is enough to share. Check ahead when bringing treats.

4. It is nearly impossible to please all children at mealtimes. I do expect children to try new foods and to eat reasonably. I do not force children to eat, but I will not allow children to skip nutritious meals and fill up at snack time. If your child is extremely fussy, you might wish to bring a sack lunch for him.

5. If a child must bring money for school lunches or activities, please put it in a sealed, marked envelope and give to me. Children love the sound and feel of money, but coins get lost, eaten, or stolen. Please do not send money with your children unless absolutely necessary.

6. Discipline your child while you are present. If you don't, I will. No jumping on furniture, running through the house, or hitting will be tolerated. If you give your child permission or allow him to leave the house while you are there, you must accept responsibility for him.

7. Family day care is special because it tries to duplicate the warmth and love of your own home. Thank you for helping me give your child the best possible care.